Pioneering Women in Martial Arts

Li T'an

ABSTRACT

Women's mixed martial arts (WMMA) is among the fastest growing sports in the world. Long existing on the margins of combat sports, women are now routinely punching, kicking, kneeing, elbowing, and strangling opponents into submission in front of sold-out crowds in the United States and around the world, as women's "cage fighting" has suddenly become a very lucrative business for combat sports promoters. Despite this, there is currently scant sociological literature on WMMA. Who are these new female subjects? In what ways are they challenging and reproducing gender? And to what extent should we characterize their participation in this new sport as empowering? My dissertation addresses these questions through a critical ethnography of WMMA. Drawing from more than four years of ethnographic fieldwork, content analysis of WMMA media, and 40 semistructured interviews with professional WMMA athletes, I offer the most thorough sociological account of WMMA to date and assess WMMA's potential as a site for the empowerment of women. I find that although women's participation in combat sports offers potential to challenge patriarchal constructions of gender and influence feminist social change, this potential is not currently being realized in WMMA. Rather, women's experiences in WMMA only seem to strengthen their beliefs in "natural" sexual difference and male superiority, as well as instill in them an ideology of individualism that blinds them to social inequality. I argue, therefore, that women's participation in WMMA does not produce outcomes consistent with feminist conceptions of empowerment. I conclude by discussing the implications of my research for women's empowerment in sport and call for a reconceptualization of empowerment that centers intersectional concerns with capitalism, white supremacy, and heteropatriarchy.

TABLE OF CONTENTS

CHAPTER I: BREAKING BARRIERS: GENDER, EMPOWERMENT, AND WOMEN'S MIXED MARTIAL ARTS

INTRODUCTION

Women's mixed martial arts (WMMA) is among the fastest growing sports in the world. Long existing on the margins of combat sports, women are now routinely punching, kicking, kneeing, elbowing, and strangling opponents into submission in front of sold-out crowds in the United States and around the world, as women's "cage fighting" has suddenly become a very lucrative business for combat sports promoters. Catapulted by the meteoric rise of WMMA superstar, Ronda Rousey, WMMA has quickly gone from being viewed as a sideshow attraction to a major professional sport in just a few years' time. As of 2018, MMA is now more popular with both men and women ages eighteen to thirty-four than major U.S. sports leagues such as the NBA, NFL, and MLB (Epstein 2018; Stainer and Master 2018), and, globally, WMMA now has a bigger fanbase than almost any other professional women's sport (Douglas 2018). While women have participated in other combat sports to varying degrees throughout history (Jennings 2014), no women's combat sport has been met with the level of curiosity and attention than that which has been given to women's mixed martial arts.

Mixed martial arts (MMA) is a full-contact combat sport that allows athletes to utilize a wide range of fighting techniques to seek victory by knockout, submission, referee intervention, or judges' decision while competing within the confines of a ring, or more commonly, a cage. Its athletes incorporate techniques from numerous martial arts disciplines—including Brazilian jiu-jitsu, muay Thai, wrestling, karate, and boxing—and wear minimal protective equipment to create the most "realistic" form of combat sport.

MMA is most commonly associated with its premier organization—Ultimate Fighting Championship (UFC)—and is colloquially referred to as "cage fighting" or "ultimate fighting" by outside observers. Although women were prohibited from competing in the UFC until 2013, women now account for more than 15% of their total roster (UFC.com) and are featured in most MMA events throughout North America and around the world.

While media coverage of WMMA has ranged from moral panic to acclaim, in recent years, WMMA has increasingly been framed as a site of women's empowerment (McClearen 2021). Drawing from popular feminist language, media have routinely portrayed WMMA athletes as revolutionaries "breaking barriers" to liberated female subjecthood through their participation in the violent and hypermasculine world of mixed martial arts. The UFC has also capitalized on this empowerment discourse, itself, with marketing taglines such as "breaking barriers" and "women's empowerment [with] a whole new look" (UFC.com) while other MMA promotions have even begun holding all-women's events, such as ONE Championship's September 2021 event, "Empower." This framing of WMMA as a site of women's empowerment raises interesting questions for the sociology of sport and the sociology of gender, as women athletes have long been viewed as "contested ideological terrain" (Messner 1988) for relations of gender and power.

While women's participation in many sports has been discussed as a source of empowerment (Blinde, Taub, and Han 1994; Hargreaves 2002; Huggins and Randell 2007; Roth and Basow 2004; Theberge 1987), women's participation in MMA is unique in that it allows women to challenge a traditional and fundamental pillar of male dominance by demonstrating women's capacity for physical violence and domination

(Mierzwinski, Velija, and Malcolm 2014). Weaving (2014), for example, argued that

WMMA athletes can counter beliefs that women are unable to engage in aggression or

risk, and that they are less physically capable than men. Quinney (2016: 53) argued,

similarly, that WMMA athletes "show fans and critics that women can be skilled in

fighting, an ideology that breaks down barriers between genders." Veit and Browning

(2021: 142), in recognizing the ways in which WMMA athletes challenge gender

stereotypes, even went as far as to characterize WMMA as an "intrinsically feminist

competition."

Despite these claims, there is currently scant sociological research on women's

mixed martial arts. The existing literature on WMMA is largely comprised of discourse

analysis (Channon et al. 2018; Chisholm, Weaving, and Bischoping 2016; McClearen

2015; McClearen 2018; Quinney 2015; Quinney 2016; Sailors and Weaving 2017;

Salvini and Marchi Júnior 2016), content analysis (Jennings 2015), and media and

cultural studies (Jakubowska, Channon, and Matthews 2016; McClearen 2021; Weaving

2014), and findings drawn from interviews with WMMA hobbyists (Channon 2014;

Channon and Jennings 2013; Mierzwinski, Velija, and Malcolm 2014). While these

studies have provided valuable insight into the business and culture of WMMA, less is

known about the lived experiences of professional WMMA athletes, themselves, and

whether such athletes are experiencing WMMA as a site of empowerment.

My dissertation begins to fill this gap through a critical ethnography of women's

mixed martial arts. Drawing from more than four years of ethnographic fieldwork, content analysis of WMMA media, and 40 semistructured interviews with professional WMMA athletes, my work builds on the insight provided by prior studies to offer a more complete picture of these women athletes' social worlds. Analyzing my data through an intersectional feminist framework, I take seriously this notion of WMMA as a site of women's empowerment and attempt to unpack what that means—not just for the athletes themselves, but also for women in general. In doing so, I ask: Are WMMA athletes *really* breaking barriers?

BACKGROUND: A BRIEF HISTORY OF WOMEN'S MIXED MARTIAL ARTS

While "No Holds Barred" (NHB) fighting existed in many forms throughout history—perhaps most notably, in "Vale Tudo" contests in Brazil—the modern sport of MMA began in 1993 with the UFC in the United States. Originally promoted with slogans such as "there are no rules" and "two men enter, one man leaves" (Walters 2015), the UFC immediately became the subject of political and social controversy, leading US Senator John McCain to famously label MMA "human cock-fighting" and push for its prohibition (Gaul 2016). But despite this initial controversy, the UFC has since grown into a multi-billion-dollar company and MMA is now regulated in all 50 United States.

While women were initially barred from competing in MMA, on March 28th, 1997, the International Fighting Championship (IFC) held the first women's mixed martial arts bout in the United States. Around this time, the first all-female mixed martial arts organizations began to appear in Japan, most notably Ladies Legend Pro-Wrestling, K-Grace, and Smackgirl (Jennings 2014). By the 2000s, several major United States mixed martial arts promotions began to feature WMMA bouts, including Hook-N-Shoot,

King of the Cage, Bodog Fight, EliteXC, Strikeforce, and Bellator. These promotions were responsible for launching the careers of several WMMA pioneers, including Marloes Coenen, Megumi Fujii, Miesha Tate, and the "first lady" of WMMA, Gina Carano (Jennings 2014).

Carano, a conventionally attractive white woman with an impressive record of accomplishment as a professional muay Thai fighter prior to her time in MMA, quickly became a star in Strikeforce, and subsequently became known as the "face of WMMA." She would eventually go on to challenge for the inaugural Strikeforce women's featherweight title but would be defeated at four minutes and fifty-nine seconds of the first round by Brazil's Cris Cyborg. Unlike Carano, whose conventionally attractive appearance made her a marketing draw, Cyborg became the subject of heavy criticism and controversy, due to her positive test for the anabolic steroid, Stanozolol, and her strong, muscular build and "masculine" traits. Cyborg subsequently became a target of UFC President, Dana White, and UFC commentator and conservative podcast host, Joe Rogan, who mocked her by suggesting that she looked like male MMA athlete, Wanderlei Silva, "in a dress and heels," and insinuating that she had a penis. Still, Cyborg would go on to become a dominant champion in both Elite XC and Strikeforce and become one of the sport's biggest draws.

In 2012, a new promotion, Invicta Fighting Championships, became the first major all-female mixed martial arts organization in the United States (Jennings 2014). Based out of Kansas City, Kansas, Invicta sought to offer a major platform for professional WMMA athletes to compete on a consistent basis, without having to accept short-notice bouts and bouts outside of their respective weight classes, as was common at the time due to the lack of participation in women's MMA (InvictaFC.com). Invicta FC President, Shannon Knapp, a longtime veteran of the combat sports world, recognized the need for a more professional outlet for WMMA competitors, informed by her experience in other MMA promotions, such as Strikeforce, King of the Cage, and WFA. Invicta quickly became home to an impressive roster of WMMA talent, and launched the careers of numerous WMMA stars, such as Michelle Waterson, Leslie Smith, and Amanda Nunes.

Despite the increased popularity and respectability of WMMA, the UFC was slow to accept women athletes into their brand. On January 19th, 2011, a reporter for the tabloid news website, TMZ, asked UFC President, Dana White, in a now infamous viral video, "When are we gonna' see women in the UFC, man? Anytime soon?" White offered a quick, one-word response: "Never." Yet, just roughly two years after White so casually dismissed women's chances of ever competing in the UFC, he signed Strikeforce champion and Judo Olympic bronze medalist, Ronda Rousey, to become the first woman to compete for the promotion. White would later credit Rousey for changing his mind about women's place in the UFC, stating in an interview with ESPN, "I was trying to get people to accept the men fighting in the cage. And I'm going to admit, you know, there's this male chauvinist side to all of us. I don't want to see a pretty girl getting elbowed in the face. Who wants to see that? I don't wanna' see that. Then, I met Ronda Rousey."

Rousey, a blond, conventionally attractive white woman with a reputation as a brash, trash-talking, violent finisher became the perfect athlete to introduce the UFC's audience to women's mixed martial arts. While similarly "marketable" (read: white and conventionally attractive) WMMA athletes such as Gina Carano and Miesha Tate had already enjoyed modest commercial success in rival promotions, Strikeforce and Elite XC, Rousey's brash demeanor and ability to finish fights in quick and dramatic fashion caught the eye of White and led to her being crowned as the UFC's first women's bantamweight champion, even before she had ever competed for the UFC. Rousey's first UFC bout would take place on February 23rd, 2013, at UFC 157, against San Diego's Liz "Girl-Rilla" Carmouche. Carmouche, a former marine known for her imposing physical strength and gritty determination would prove a tough challenge for Rousey but would ultimately succumb to Rousey's signature armbar submission hold at four minutes and forty-nine seconds of the first round. The bout would mark the beginning of what came to be known as the "Rousey era" which saw Rousey grow from a relative unknown to one of the biggest stars in the history of women's sports.

Following the win over Carmouche, Rousey would go on to host the 18th season of the UFC's *Ultimate Fighter* reality TV show alongside her longtime rival, Miesha Tate. Rousey and Tate had previously competed against each other in Strikeforce in March of 2012, with Rousey defeating Tate via her trademark armbar, and subsequently breaking Tate's arm. The rivalry would lead to many heated exchanges on the show, with Rousey capitalizing on every opportunity to antagonize her rival. The show would also serve as the first *Ultimate Fighter* season to feature women competitors. While the

Ultimate Fighter is widely regarded as having played a significant role in the growth of both the UFC and MMA, the show's first 17 seasons exclusively featured male competitors and coaches. For the show's 18th season, male and female competitors would live and train alongside one another in the *Ultimate Fighter* house while competing in their respective gendered divisions. And while the season debuted to just 762,000 viewers—at the time, the lowest season debut in the series' history (Wilcox 2013)—the show was responsible for introducing many UFC fans to WMMA for the first time and building Rousey into one of the biggest UFC stars in the promotion's history.

Following the completion of the show, Rousey and Tate faced off once again in a highly anticipated rematch, with Rousey yet again securing victory with her signature armbar. Rousey would go on to defend her title four more times, defeating contenders, Sara McMann, Alexis Davis, Cat Zingano, and Bethe Correia, along the way. During this time, Rousey would grow into a media superstar, securing acting roles in notable films such as The Expendables 3 (2014), Furious 7 (2015), and Entourage (2015). In November of 2015, however, Rousey would face her toughest challenge to date against New Mexico's Holly "The Preacher's Daughter" Holm.

Holm—at the time, undefeated in 9 professional MMA bouts—was a former boxing champion with an impressive record of 33-2. Holm's soft-spoken demeanor served as a stark contrast to Rousey's brashness, as did her striking-heavy style when compared with Rousey's Judo-based grappling approach. Leading up to the fight, the UFC released a promotional video that portrayed the two women's lives from their first experience with martial arts as young girls up to their present-day contest (see McClearen

2018 for a detailed analysis). The video was widely acclaimed for its powerful visuals and narrative (see, for example, Martin 2015), and contributed to the Rousey-Holm contest becoming one of the top 3 best-selling pay-per-view events in UFC history, as well as the UFC's fourth most successful live gate of all time (Popkin 2015).

In the contest between Rousey and Holm, to the surprise of many, Holm—a huge betting underdog—would immediately gain the upper hand, breaking Rousey's jaw with a straight left hand in the bout's opening seconds. The remainder of the round saw Rousey unsuccessfully trying to corner her opponent while Holm used her savvy footwork to evade Rousey's attacks while continuing to land powerful punches. When the round ended, an exhausted Rousey returned to her corner with blood dripping from her mouth. As Rousey attempted to collect herself while listening to instructions from her head coach, Edmond Tarverdyan, UFC commentators, Joe Rogan and Mike Goldberg, commented on Rousey's battered and tired appearance. "In all likelihood," Goldberg declared, "that is the first round that Ronda has lost in her professional career."

As the second round started, things continued to get worse for Rousey, with the round's opening seconds producing a memorable moment as Holm ducked under a Rousey left hook, forcing Rousey to lose her balance and stumble into the cage wall. Moments later, Holm landed another powerful left hand that sent Rousey to the canvas. As Rousey made her way back to her feet, Holm timed a perfectly placed kick against the side of Rousey's head that rendered her unconscious. Holm immediately pounced on the fallen Rousey, landing a series of hammer fists that forced referee, Herb Dean, to waive off the contest and declare Holm the new UFC women's bantamweight champion.

After the bout, things only got worse for Rousey, as her past comments and refusal to congratulate Holm on her victory made her an unsympathetic figure in the eyes of the public. A few days later, reporters would catch up to Rousey in the Los Angeles International Airport as she returned to her hometown of Los Angeles where she was seen covering her face with a pillow and refusing to answer questions. The image of Rousey hiding behind a pillow quickly spread online and she immediately became the subject of numerous internet memes that reveled in her defeat. For the next several months, Rousey would largely avoid the media, drawing continued ire from fans who once supported her and now labeled her a bad sport.

In her first television appearance after the defeat, Rousey was featured as a guest on *The Ellen DeGeneres Show*. Rousey, wearing a tight-fitting, low-cut dress and a full face of makeup, would offer a series of excuses for her loss before DeGeneres asked, "Did you worry for a minute, like, could this be permanent? Did I really hurt myself and maybe I won't do this again?" "No, to be honest, what I was thinking…" Rousey responded, trying unsuccessfully to hold back tears,

> Honestly, my thought, I was like…I was like in the medical room and I was like down in the corner and I was like, "What am I anymore if I'm not this?" I was literally sitting there and like thinking about killing myself and then that exact second I'm like, "I'm nothing. What do I do anymore?" And, like, no one gives a shit about me anymore without this. To be honest, I looked up and I saw my man—Travis was standing there—and I looked up at him and just was like, "I need to have his babies. I need to stay alive."

The comment drew an applause from the predominantly female audience, as well as from DeGeneres herself.

Just a few months after defeating Rousey and becoming the UFC women's bantamweight champion, Holm would defend her title for the first time against Rousey's longtime rival, Miesha Tate. Over the course of the first four rounds, Holm would largely control the action and was presumed to be up three rounds to one heading into the bout's final round. With just two minutes remaining in the fight, Tate secured a takedown against the champion, Holm. In a rush to get back to her feet, Holm exposed her back to Tate and was subsequently strangled unconscious in a shocking upset defeat.

Following her victory, Tate would make her first title defense against Brazil's Amanda Nunes. The contest would prove uncompetitive, as Nunes secured a rear naked strangle at just three minutes and sixteen seconds into the opening round. With the victory, Nunes would become the UFC's first openly gay champion.

Nunes' first title defense would come against the former champion, Ronda Rousey, in Rousey's first fight back since losing her title to Holly Holm. Leading up to the bout, Rousey would once again draw the ire of the UFC's fanbase, as she refused to participate in her pre-fight media obligations, as is typically required of all UFC athletes. "When I try and do favors and make everybody else happy," Rousey explained, "at the end of the day, they walk away happy and I'm the one who has to deal with the depression. All the pay-per-views in the world, all the money in the world, it means fucking nothing to me because I lost" (Okamoto 2016). Somewhat uncharacteristically, UFC President, Dana White, would defend Rousey's media refusal, explaining, "Everybody knows how I feel about Ronda. She worked harder than anybody for years, and she needed a break. Now that she's coming back, I'm kind of letting her do it on her terms." The double standard drew criticism from MMA fans and media members alike who saw the UFC's handling of the situation as evidence of favoritism toward Rousey. This criticism grew louder following the release of the promotional video for the Rousey-Nunes contest which overwhelmingly focused on Rousey's return and only briefly showed Nunes, despite the fact that Nunes was now the UFC champion.

Leading up the bout, MMA media members, such as Ariel Helwani, questioned whether Rousey was truly ready to return, as her unwillingness to discuss her loss with the MMA media was seen as evidence that she had still not recovered from her shocking defeat. These concerns would prove not without merit as the bout's opening seconds saw Rousey freeze after being struck with a stiff jab from the champion and quickly retreat after being struck again by a subsequent combination of punches. Nunes quickly pounced on the vulnerable former champion, attacking Rousey with a barrage of unanswered strikes until referee, Herb Dean, waived the contest off at just 48 seconds of the first round, declaring Nunes the victor.

As medical officials quickly attended to Rousey, Nunes paced around the cage holding up her index finger to her mouth, as if to "shoosh" any detractors who anticipated a competitive contest. In her post-fight interview with UFC commentator, Joe Rogan, Nunes declared, "[Rousey] had her time. She did a lot for this sport. Thank you, Ronda Rousey. But, right now, I'm the champion and I'm here to stay. People, let's stop this Ronda Rousey nonsense. Okay? I'm the champion here, Amanda Nunes, 'The Lioness.'" Rogan followed up by asking, "What was it like going through the training camp for this and knowing that so much of the promotion was on Ronda and very little of it was paying

attention to you when you were the champion?" Nunes responded,

> I love that. When I asked for this fight, I [knew] everything, you know? I prepared
> my mind. I prepared my spirit and my body for this moment. I know Ronda
> Rousey's bigger. I know they love Ronda Rousey. But, nobody's gonna' take this
> belt from me. In my whole camp, I [knew] already the promotion's gonna' be
> everything about her. I'm really ready for this fight so badly. I [knew] I was
> gonna' beat the shit out of Ronda Rousey for a long time. I told you. I trained for
> this girl since my first fight in UFC. I know it's gonna' happen. Now, tonight, I
> prove to everybody I'm the best on the planet. Come on, guys! Are you serious?
> Do you guys understand? Bullshit Ronda Rousey. Come on! Now, she's gonna'
> retire and go do movies. She already has a lot of money. Come on. We have, in
> this division, we have a lot of talent. You know? Now, you guys have to look at
> these girls coming up working hard. Come on. Forget about Ronda Rousey.

Following the bout, Rousey would in fact retire, and would eventually transition to

professional wrestling.

In April 2021, Rousey announced that she was pregnant with her husband, Travis

Browne's, child, declaring that the "baddest baby on the planet" was on its way (King

2021). Nunes, on the other hand, would continue her reign as UFC women's

bantamweight champion while also managing to capture (and defend) a second UFC title

along the way. Throughout this time, WMMA would continue to grow in popularity, with

WMMA athletes now comprising some of the biggest stars in women's sports.

SIGNIFICANCE

The Political and Cultural Significance of WMMA

In recent years, mixed martial arts has become a site of rising political and

cultural significance. While for much of its history, MMA was considered a niche sport,

the recent success of the UFC in the United States has moved MMA to the forefront of

popular sports culture. UFC commentator, Joe Rogan, for example, has used his popularity among MMA fans to grow his podcast, "The Joe Rogan Experience," into the number one podcast in the world. In May of 2020, Rogan signed an exclusive deal with Spotify, reportedly for more than 200 million dollars, making it one of the largest licensing deals in podcast history (Rosman et al. 2022). The massive success of Rogan's podcast has allowed him to play an outsized role in American politics and popular culture, making him one of the most influential people in the world. In May of 2021, *The New York Times* published an article, entitled, "Joe Rogan Is Too Big To Cancel," calling Rogan "one of the most consumed media products on the planet with the power to shape tastes, politics, [and] medical decisions" (Flegenheimer 2021). Indeed, Rogan has repeatedly made headlines for his stances against "wokeness," "cancel culture," and vaccines, garnering him favor from those on the political right. In October of 2021, for instance, Fox News' Laura Ingraham praised Rogan as an example of a "manly man" on her show, *The Ingraham Angle,* as she claimed that liberals were "feminizing men" (Anglesey 2021). In November of 2021, US Senator Ted Cruz suggested that if Texas were to secede from the United States, Joe Rogan could be the state's President (Cohen 2021). Such framing has allowed Rogan to represent, perhaps more so than anyone else in the United States, contemporary white masculinity.

In 2020, the popularity of Rogan's podcast became so great that he was seriously discussed as a host for a Presidential debate between candidates Donald Trump and Joe Biden—an offer Trump accepted (Wulfsohn 2020). This was just one instance of Rogan's outsized influence on contemporary American politics. Rogan has also played a big role in bolstering the careers of several far-right activists, including Alex Jones, Milo

Yiannopoulos, and Gavin McInnes. Alex Jones, in particular—a far-right conspiracy

theorist who has argued that the 2012 Sandy Hook Elementary School Mass Shooting

was a hoax and that several high-ranking Democratic Party officials were involved in a

human trafficking and child sex ring—has benefitted enormously from being featured as

a guest on "The Joe Rogan Experience," as his repeated appearances on the podcast have

made him a favorite among Rogan's loyal listeners. Jones' website, *InfoWars.com*, now

receives approximately 10 million monthly visits, making its reach greater than many

mainstream news websites such as *The Economist* and *Newsweek* (Beauchamp 2016).

Other far-right activists have repeatedly aligned themselves with Rogan's politics and

have used Rogan's popularity to bolster support for their individual brands. In April of

2021, for example, Congresswoman Lauren Boebert tweeted, "Why is Joe Rogan not

allowed to give medical opinions but Bill Gates is?" The tweet received nearly thirty-five

thousand "likes" and was shared over six thousand times. In August of 2021, Donald

Trump Jr. tweeted a video of Rogan claiming that vaccine requirements would move the

United States "one step closer" to a dictatorship (Ankel 2021). As of November 2021, the

video had received over four million views. Such instances are illustrative of Rogan's

place in American political culture.

The UFC, itself, has also been at the forefront of American political culture.

While, in its early days, the UFC received condemnation from politicians on both sides of

the political aisle, in recent years, conservatives have actually begun using the UFC and

the sport of MMA as a platform to spread right-wing ideologies and bolster support for

the Republican party (Zidan 2020a). Donald Trump, for example, has utilized his friendship with UFC President, Dana White, very effectively to garner support from UFC fans and athletes (Zidan 2020a). In 2016 and 2020, White served as a guest speaker at the Republican National Convention and was a major donor to Trump's Presidential campaign (Graham 2020). In 2018, in an effort to bolster support for Trump's reelection, the UFC released a documentary on their streaming service, *UFC Fight Pass,* entitled, "Combatant in Chief," which told the story of Trump's influence on the UFC, as well as on the sport of MMA. In 2019, Trump actually appeared at a UFC event as White's guest, becoming the first sitting President to ever do so (Graham 2020). In May of 2020, in a truly unprecedented move, the UFC began its UFC 249 pay-per-view broadcast with a pre-recorded video of Trump, in which he gave a brief speech congratulating White on the UFC's first pay-per-view event since the start of the COVID-19 pandemic (Segura 2020). In the video, Trump states,

> I want to congratulate Dana White and the UFC. They're going to have a big match. We love it. We think it's important. Get the sports leagues back. Let's play. We do the social distancing and whatever else you have to do but we need sports. We want our sports back, and congratulations to Dana White and the UFC.

Such statements are an example of the way in which Trump and other right-wing politicians have repeatedly used their support of MMA and the UFC to construct themselves as being "pro sports" and garner support from male voters (Vescio and Schermerhorn 2021).

The UFC has also promoted far-right politicians such as Candace Owens at their events and in their promotional materials (Nightingale 2021). In a promotional video for the February 2021 event, "UFC 258: Usman vs. Burns," for example, Owens was briefly shown attending a prior UFC event, accompanied by the title, "political activist." Owens, herself, has also featured UFC athletes Colby Covington and Beneil Dariush on her show, *The Candace Owens Show,* and used her association with the UFC to build a following among MMA fans. Covington immediately caught the eye of Owens after he began portraying himself as an ardent supporter of Donald Trump by frequently wearing a "Make America Great Again" hat and declaring himself "Donald Trump's favorite fighter" (Campbell 2019). Covington, in fact, was even invited to the White House to meet then-President Trump, following his victory over UFC veteran, Raphael Dos Anjos at UFC 225 (Campbell 2019). Dariush caught Owens' attention after his bizarre post-fight speech following his victory over Tony Ferguson at UFC 262, in which he dedicated his victory to "all the people who've been hurt by Marxist ideologies" and called on Elon Musk to send him a new car (Samano 2021). Other UFC athletes such as Michael Chandler have also participated in political events alongside Owens, as well as alongside other far-right figures such as Tucker Carlson and Donald Trump Jr. (Zidan 2021b).

Several other notable MMA athletes have also begun playing an active role in American politics since the start of the COVID-19 pandemic. In October of 2020, former UFC title challenger, Jorge Masvidal, participated in a four-part "Fighters Against Socialism" bus tour hosted by Donald Trump Jr. and the Trump re-election campaign, where he spoke about the "horrors" of communism and socialism (Zidan 2020a). The same month, former UFC interim champion, Colby Covington, participated in a pro-Trump boat parade, alongside Eric Trump. On December 7th, 2020, former UFC light heavyweight champion, Tito Ortiz, became the first high-profile MMA athlete to be sworn in as an elected member of the United States government, where he served as Mayor Pro Tem on Huntington Beach, California's City Council (Fry and Miller 2021). Ortiz's tenure would be short lived, as he resigned from his position in May of 2021, citing a sustained "character assassination" effort and fears for the safety of his family (Fry and Miller 2021). During his tenure, Ortiz was the subject of frequent criticism, as he routinely flouted mask rules and was a vocal supporter of the QAnon conspiracy cult, and at one point even suggested that members of the Black Lives Matter movement were planning a trip to Huntington Beach to "burn [the] city down and rape [Huntington Beach citizens'] wives" (Bergengruen 2021; Palmer 2021).

MMA athletes such as Ortiz have also played an outsized role in the spread of conspiracy theories during the COVID-19 pandemic (Silverman and Khan 2020). Since the start of the pandemic, numerous MMA athletes have pushed conspiracy theories ranging from claims that the COVID-19 pandemic was an elaborate hoax orchestrated by the United States government as a means to confiscate American citizens' guns to those even suggesting that the 2020 murder of George Floyd was a setup by the Biden administration to garner support among Black voters (Zidan 2020b). Perhaps, no MMA athlete has garnered more attention for their role in the spread of COVID-19 conspiracy theories than the "first lady" of WMMA, Gina Carano. Carano, a cross-over star known for her role in the television series, *The Mandalorian,* in addition to her career in MMA, was fired from her role in the series after likening the experience of Jews during the Holocaust to that of conservatives in the contemporary United States (Parker and Couch 2021). She was subsequently hired by conservative political commentator and podcast host, Ben Shapiro, for a movie project with his website, *The Daily Wire.* In a statement

for *Deadline.com*, Carano announced,

> *The Daily Wire* is helping make one of my dreams—to develop and produce my
> own film—come true. I cried out and my prayer was answered. I am sending out a
> direct message of hope to everyone living in fear of cancellation by the
> totalitarian mob. I have only just begun using my voice which is now freer than
> ever before, and I hope it inspires others to do the same. They can't cancel us if
> we don't let them (Wiseman 2021).

But Carano isn't the only WMMA athlete to make headlines since the start of the

pandemic. In addition to Carano, several other WMMA athletes have also made headlines

for their anti-social behavior and alignment with far-right politics. WMMA pioneer, Tara

LaRosa, for example, became the subject of public scrutiny after declaring her support

for the far-right fascist group, The Proud Boys, and claiming to be a member (Zidan

2021a). LaRosa, a veteran of 27 professional fights, began attending right-wing protests

following her retirement in 2015 and, in 2018, spoke at a #HimToo event that was

organized by members of the far-right fascist group, Patriot Prayer (Zidan 2021a). In

2019, a video surfaced online of LaRosa pinning an anti-Trump demonstrator to the

ground and sitting on her chest as the woman cried out, "I can't breathe," to which

LaRosa responded, "I don't care" (Zidan 2021a). In late 2020, LaRosa established a

channel on the encrypted messenger app, Telegram, entitled, "Proud Girls USA." The

same day, the "ProudBoysUSA" channel voiced their displeasure, stating, "Don't ride our

coattails. Want to support us? Get married, have babies, and take care of your family"

(Reid Ross 2020). LaRosa would respond by posting a picture of herself alongside Proud

Boys leader, Enrique Tarrio, and declaring herself tougher than "99%" of the men

voicing their displeasure (Reid Ross 2020).

MMA's ties to right-wing politics are also not unique to the United States. Several far-right politicians outside of the U.S. have also begun using MMA athletes to bolster support for their political brands—most notably, in Eastern Europe. Chechen dictator, Ramzan Kadyrov, for instance, has repeatedly used now-retired former UFC lightweight champion, Khabib Nurmagomedov, as a geopolitical tool to strengthen efforts to expand Chechnya into Nurmagomedov's home country of Dagestan (Zidan 2019a). Kadyrov has also paid other high-profile MMA stars, such as former UFC welterweight champion, Kamaru Usman, and former UFC middleweight champion, Chris Weidman, to attend his Akhmat MMA fight club as a means to curry political favor. Kadyrov has also met with several other UFC athletes, including Frank Mir, Fabricio Werdum, Frankie Edgar, Alexander Gustafsson, Ilir Latifi, Makwan Amirkhani, and Khamzat Chimaev, as well as other notable combat sports athletes such as Renzo Gracie, Badr Hari, Floyd Mayweather, Roy Jones Jr., and Mike Tyson (Zidan 2020c). As explained by MMA journalist, Karim Zidan,

> By associating with some of the most popular figures in combat sports, Kadyrov presents an image of a benevolent, sports-loving leader rather than a cruel tyrant. This tactic is known as sportswashing—a term coined by Amnesty International in 2018 to describe authoritarian regimes using sports to whitewash their human rights records—and has been especially useful in cementing [Kadyrov's] rule in Chechnya (Zidan 2020c).

Kadyrov, himself, has been accused of numerous human rights abuses ranging from "torture" to "extra judicial killings" (Zidan 2020c). Many of these killings were reportedly against gay men in what has been described as a "gay purge" in the Chechen Republic (Taylor 2017). In an interview with HBO reporter, David Scott, for the show, "Real Sports with Bryant Gumbel," Kadyrov, when asked about the accusations of violence against the LGBTQ+ community, responded, "This is nonsense. We don't have

those kinds of people here. We don't have any gays. If there are any, take them to

Canada. Praise be to God. Take them far from us so we don't have them at home. To

purify our blood, if there are any here, take them (Scott 2017).

On December 20th, 2017, the United States Treasury Department imposed

sanctions against Kadyrov, as well as the Akhmat MMA fight club and the Kadyrov-

controlled fight promotion, Absolute Championship Akhmat. On December 10th, 2020,

the U.S. Treasury Department announced a series of new sanctions on Kadyrov for

"numerous gross violations of human rights" (Hansler and Gaouette 2020). In an official

statement, then-Secretary of State, Mike Pompeo, wrote,

> Today's action serves to notify Mr. Kadyrov that his involvement in gross
> violations of human rights has consequences, both for him and his family, and
> that the United States is committed to using all the tools at our disposal to ensure
> accountability for those who engage in this abhorrent behavior.

But despite the credible accusations of Kadyrov's human rights abuses and the

subsequent sanctions against him, incredibly, Kadyrov was actually featured on the UFC

242 broadcast as he was pictured cheering on Dagastani fighter, Khabib Nurmagomedov,

from the front row of The Arena, Yas Island in Abu Dhabi, United Arab Emirates.

According to Zidan (2019b), this appearance allowed Kadyrov to both strengthen ties and

enhance bilateral relations with the United Arab Emirates as well as rebrand himself and

his republic to his neighbors in the North Caucasus.

In November of 2021, *VICE* published a short documentary, entitled, *Inside a

Neo-Nazi Fight Club*, about the growing far-right extremism movement within MMA.

The documentary details the ways in which right-wing extremists have increasingly begun using MMA to draw people into far-right and white supremacist ideologies while

training them with fighting skills in preparation for them to enact political violence.

According to the documentary, over the past ten years, several far-right MMA

promotions around the world have actually begun staging "whites-only" MMA events

and pushing a "racist, hypermasculine ideology" to their supporters. These promotions

include Kampf Der Nibelungen and White Rex in Russia, Pride France in France, Pro-

Patria in Greece, and the Rise Above Movement in the United States. According to the

documentary, the key player among these groups is White Rex.

The documentary states that White Rex was founded in 2008 as a far-right

clothing label by the Russian neo-Nazi hooligan, Denis Kapustin, who is widely known

by his pseudonym, Denis Nikitin. According to the documentary, White Rex markets

itself, not just as a fight promotion, but also an "all-encompassing lifestyle brand," by

selling active gear and weaponry. As explained by the documentary's narrator, Tim

Hume,

> White nationalist politics [are] central to the brand's identity, with graphics
> depicting the consonants in White Rex as standing for "White Heterosexual
> Reactionary Xenophobe" while its social media pages express support for the so-
> called "14 words,"—the white supremacist slogan about "securing the future of
> the white race."

According to Robert Claus, author of *Their Fight: How Europe's Extreme Right Is

Training for the Overthrow* (2020), White Rex appeals to a "very traditional, in their

understanding, natural interpretation of masculinity" (VICE 2021). According to far-right

researcher, Pavel Klymenko, its efforts can be described as,

> neo-Nazi propaganda done with…skills in design [and] marketing…The image
> that is constructed is that of a warrior that is always ready to fight using some sort

of Nordic symbolism, and they believe that they need to defend something. Some
of them define it as Christianity. Some of them define it as white European
heritage. Others are just protesting or revolting against the modern world (VICE
2021).

These efforts have not only been successful in building White Rex's brand in Russia, but

also in influencing the development of "copycat" promotions such as the Rise Above

Movement in the United States. Based in Southern California, the Rise Above Movement

was started by an American far-right activist named Robert Rundo (VICE 2021).

According to MMA journalist, Karim Zidan, Rundo is "one of the most dangerous white

supremacists currently active in the mixed martial arts space" (VICE 2021). Billing itself

as the "premier MMA club of the alt-right," the Rise Above Movement claimed at one

point to have over 50 members and links with far-right groups in Europe before four of

its members, including Rundo, were charged with inciting a riot in Huntington Beach,

California, after attacking counter-demonstrators at a pro-Trump rally (VICE 2021).

Rundo currently hosts a podcast with White Rex's Denis Nikitin which provides listeners

with guidance on how to set up their own white supremacist fight clubs (VICE 2021).

MMA's culture of far-right politics, white supremacy, and hypermasculinity

stands in stark contrast to its framing as a space of women's empowerment. While

WMMA athletes are undoubtedly acquiring impressive physical skills, it is unclear

whether the acquisition of these skills can be characterized as an "empowering"

experience for these athletes, themselves, nor is it clear if the benefits gained through

these athletes' MMA training extend to women as a collective group. To situate this new

sport within broader discussions of women's empowerment, I now turn to the academic

literature on women's empowerment and sport.

LITERATURE REVIEW

Women's Empowerment and Sport

Numerous scholars have discussed the "empowerment" potential of women's sports (Blinde, Taub, and Han 1993; Blinde, Taub, and Han 1994; Channon and Phipps 2017; Hargreaves 1997; Hargreaves 1999; Huggins and Randell 2007; Liechty, Willfong, and Sveinson 2016; Lim and Dixon 2017; Migliaccio and Berg 2007; Paul and Blank 2015; Pelak 2002; Rana 2017; Roth and Basow 2004; Theberge 1987; Theberge 2003; Velija, Mierzwinski, and Fortune 2013; Wedgwood 2004; Willson et al. 2017). Hope for this potential has rested on women athletes' ability to "break barriers" to liberated female subjecthood by participating in activities that have traditionally been associated with male bodies and masculinities, and sport's ability to "reduc[e] [the] physical power imbalances on which patriarchy is founded and reified" (Castelnuovo and Guthrie 1998: 13). Among the first to conceptualize sports as a site of women's empowerment was Nancy Theberge. Theberge (1987: 393) contended that sports provided a setting to "explore the content of the bodily aspect of women's existence." She argued further that sports represented a setting in which women could begin to unravel the social and cultural expressions of the physical differences between women and men. The "liberatory possibility" of sports, she concluded, "lies in the opportunity for women to experience the creativity and energy of their bodily power and to develop this power in the community of women" (Theberge 1987: 393).

Michael Messner was also one of the first scholars to discuss sports as a site of women's empowerment. Messner (1988: 198) argued that women's participation in sport represented a quest by women for equality, control of their bodies, and self-definition, and as such presented a challenge to the "ideological basis of male domination." Because sports serve as a primary institutional means for bolstering the ideology of male superiority, he argued, women athletes represent "contested ideological terrain" for challenging and legitimizing the unequal power relations between women and men in society (Messner 1988: 198). While rejecting the notion that women's increased athleticism unambiguously signaled increased freedom and equality for women, he argued that "equal opportunity" for women athletes marked a shift in the ideological hegemony of male dominance and superiority. He recognized, however, that other social factors—such as the male-dominant structure of organized sports and the patriarchal media framing of women athletes—presented obstacles for any fundamental challenge to male hegemony. He concluded therefore that, "it remains for a critical feminist theory to recognize the emergent contradictions in this system in order to inform a liberating social practice" (Messner 1988: 208).

According to Burke (2019), ethnographic and interview-based studies of women's sports have revealed the following consistent themes of empowerment, freedom, and individual choice for women athletes:

1. The opportunity to participate in teams that produce "family-like" relationships based in trust and interpersonal support (Liechty, Willfong, and Sveinson 2016; Migliaccio and Berg 2007; Paul and Blank 2015)

2. The opportunity to work with a diverse group of women who share a common cause, partly centered around the origin and sustainability of the team and the

league (Liechty, Willfong, and Sveinson 2016; Migliaccio and Berg 2007; Pelak 2002; Wedgwood 2004; Willson et al. 2017)

3. The opportunity to act aggressively and engage in physicality in ways that have traditionally been denied to women, and in ways that female participants experience as personally enjoyable and pleasurable (Channon and Phipps 2017; Liechty, Willfong, and Sveinson 2016; Migliaccio and Berg 2007; Paul and Blank 2015; Roth and Basow 2004; Theberge 2003; Velija, Mierzwinski, and Fortune 2013)

4. The potential to develop a new style or discourse of play that emanates from the female experience (Pelak 2002; Theberge 2003)

5. The opportunity to build bodies that are capable of exhibiting physical qualities, such as strength and power, that have been traditionally associated with male bodies (Liechty, Willfong, and Sveinson 2016; Migliaccio and Berg 2007; Theberge 2003; Velija, Mierzwinski, and Fortune 2013; Wedgwood 2004).

While such studies have revealed numerous benefits to women's participation in sport, definitions and indicators of empowerment within this body of research have remained elusive and rare (Bunsell 2013). According to Mosedale (2005), while a consensus definition of empowerment has yet to be reached, there are four aspects of empowerment which seem to be generally accepted in the women's empowerment literature:

1. To be empowered, one must have been disempowered. Women, as a group, are disempowered relative to men.

2. Empowerment cannot be bestowed by a third party. Rather, those who would become empowered must claim it. Women, therefore, must claim empowerment for themselves.

3. Reflection, analysis, and action are involved in the process of empowerment which may happen on an individual or collective level.

4. Empowerment is an ongoing process rather than a product. One does not arrive at a stage of being empowered in an absolute sense. Women are empowered, or disempowered, relative to others or relative to themselves at a previous time.

Central to definitions and indicators of empowerment within this body of research are conceptions of power. According to Mosedale (2005), within the social sciences, power has typically been conceived of as "power over," wherein one has power over another to the extent that they can get the other to do something they would not otherwise do. In this model, power is a "zero-sum game," wherein one person's gain is another's loss. This stands in contrast to other forms of power, such as "power within," "power to," and "power with." "Power within," according to Mosedale (2005: 250), refers to "assets" such as "self-esteem" and "self-confidence." "Power to," refers to that which increases the boundaries of what is achievable for any particular person or group. "Power with," refers to collective action, "recognizing that more can be achieved by a group acting together than by individuals alone" (Mosedale 2005: 250).

Mosedale (2005) engages Foucault's (1990) model of power, wherein power is understood to circulate and be exercised among actors through social interaction rather truly "possessed" by individuals for any fixed length of time, to stress the importance of "resistance" as an accompaniment to power. According to Mosedale (2005), the exploration of women's day-to-day experience of and resistance to power relations has been productive both in demonstrating the diverse sources of women's subjugation and in celebrating and spreading resistance to male domination. She cites consciousness-raising groups as an example of the political utility of uncovering these experiences as a means to raise awareness of women's subjugation and spread resistance to patriarchal control. The feminist assertion, "the personal is political" (Hanisch 1969), she argues, was part of the process of recognizing that power was exercised in personal relationships as well as in more public arenas.

In Mosedale's (2005) model of women's empowerment, power is understood to contain both structural and individual components. As explained by Mosedale (2005: 251), her model

> accept[s] that group membership constrains a person's possibilities and defines some boundaries, which being socially constructed can therefore be changed. The extent to which an individual presses against, or accepts, these boundaries and the extent to which change is possessed (and the power of those opposing it) all contribute to the shape and durability of these boundaries.

She goes on to state that she recognizes that people have more or less power depending on their specific situation and that they can be relatively powerless in one situation and relatively powerful in another. On a micro level, she understands each person to exist at the center of their own space of "freedom," a space "defined by, and defining, the shifting contours of the multiple containers which circumscribe their lives" (Mosedale 2005: 251). Mosedale (2005: 252), therefore, defines women's empowerment as "the process by which women redefine and extend what is possible for them to be and do in situations where they have been restricted, compared to men, from being and doing." "Alternatively," she continues, "women's empowerment is the process by which women redefine gender roles in ways which extend their possibilities for being and doing."

While Mosedale's (2005) definition of empowerment is widely cited in the women's empowerment literature, other scholars, too, have proposed useful definitions. Kabeer (1999: 437), for example, in what is, perhaps, the most widely cited paper in the women's empowerment literature, defines empowerment as "the process by which those who have been denied the ability to make strategic life choices acquire such an ability." Indeed, the notion of "choice" is central to Kabeer's (1999) understanding of power. Kabeer (1999) acknowledges, however, that the equation of choice with power makes it difficult to accommodate forms of gender inequality that appear to result from the choices of women, themselves, such as women's acceptance of secondary claims on household resources, their acquiescence to violence at the hands of their male partners, or their willingness to bear children to the detriment of their own health and survival. Such "choices," according to Kabeer (1999), constitute women's elective undermining of their own well-being and are examples of behavior in which women's internalization of their own lesser status in society leads them to discriminate against other women and girls. As stated by Kabeer (1999: 441), "While these forms of behaviour could be said to reflect 'choice,' they are also choices which stem from, and serve to reinforce, women's subordinate status."

In recognizing the limitations of choice as a proxy for power, Kabeer (1999)

arrives at a discussion of "false consciousness." False consciousness, for Kabeer (1999:

441), is not a particularly useful concept for discussions of women's empowerment, as it

implies the need to distinguish between false and "authentic" states of consciousness,

both of which Kabeer rejects. She explains,

> The consciousness we are talking about is not "false" as such since how people
> perceive their needs and interests is shaped by their individual histories and
> everyday realities, by the material and social contexts of their experiences and by
> the vantage point for reflexivity which this provides. In any situation, some needs
> and interests are self-evident, emerging out of the routine practices of daily life
> and differentiated by gender inasmuch as the responsibilities and routines of daily
> life are gender-differentiated. However, there are other needs and interests which
> do not have this self-evident nature because they derive from a "deeper" level of
> reality, one which is not evident in daily life because it is inscribed in the taken-
> for-granted rule, norms and customs within which everyday life is conducted
> (Kabeer 1999: 441).

Kabeer utilizes Bourdieu's (1977) concept of "doxa"—the aspects of tradition and culture

which are so taken-for-granted that they have become naturalized—to move away from

the authentic-false dichotomy and toward a deeper level of analysis concerned with

"differing levels of reality and the practical and strategic interests to which they give rise"

(Kabeer 1999: 441). The passage from "doxa" to discourse—a more critical

consciousness—she explains, only becomes possible when competing ways of "being

and doing" become available as material and cultural possibilities, so that "common

sense" cultural propositions begin to lose their "naturalized" character, revealing the

underlying arbitrariness of the given social order. The availability of alternatives at the

discursive level, she argues, is crucial to the emergence of a critical consciousness, which

she defines as "the process by which people move from a position of unquestioning acceptance of the social order to a critical perspective on it" (Kabeer 1999: 441). Kabeer (1999) stresses, therefore, that in assessing whether women's individual outcomes embody meaningful "choice," one should consider whether other choices were not only materially possible but whether they were conceived to be possible within a given culture.

Kabeer's (1999) discussion of culture leads her to a discussion of the importance of collective solidarity to the project of women's empowerment. She argues that in contexts where cultural values constrain women's ability to make strategic life choices, structural inequalities cannot be addressed by individuals alone. She explains that while individual women may indeed transgress cultural expectations, the impact of these transgressions on the situation of women in general is likely to be limited. Further, individual transgressive women may even pay a price for their individual autonomy. She argues, therefore, that the project of women's empowerment depends on collective solidarity as well as on individual resistance.

Kabeer (1999) highlights the interdependence of individual and structural change in processes of empowerment. She argues that structures shape individual resources, agency, and achievements, and define the parameters within which different categories of actors are able to pursue their interests. She argues that such structures also shape individual interests so that how people define their goals and what they value will reflect their social positioning as well as their individual histories, tastes, and preferences. Kabeer (1999: 462) ultimately stops short of prescribing ways to measure women's empowerment, however, as she argues that human agency is "indeterminate and hence unpredictable in a way that is antithetical to requirements of measurement." As she

explains,

> To attempt to predict at the outset of an intervention precisely how it will change
> women's lives, without some knowledge of ways of "being and doing" which are
> realizable and valued by women in that context, runs into the danger of
> prescribing the process of empowerment and thereby violating its essence, which
> is to enhance women's capacity for self-determination (Kabeer 1999: 462).

Batliwala (1994) identifies the goals of women's empowerment as challenging

patriarchal ideology; transforming the structures and institutions that reinforce and

perpetuate gender discrimination and social inequality; and enabling poor women to gain

access to, and control of, both material and informational resources. The process of this

empowerment, Batliwala argues, therefore must address all relevant structures and

sources of power. In order to challenge their subordination, Batliwala (1994: 131) argues

that women must first "recognize the ideology that legitimates male domination and

understand how it perpetuates their oppression." As she explains,

> This recognition requires reversal of the values and attitudes, indeed the entire
> worldview, that most women have internalized since earliest childhood. Women
> have been led to participate in their own oppression through a complex web of
> religious sanctions, social and cultural taboos and superstitions, hierarchies
> among women in the family...behavioral training, seclusion, veiling, curtailment
> of physical mobility, discrimination in food and other family sources, and control
> of their sexuality...Because questioning is not allowed, the majority of women
> grow up believing that this is the just and "natural" order (Batliwala 1994: 131).

Batliwala (1994: 131-132) contends, therefore, that the demand for change does not

usually begin spontaneously from the condition of subjugation but rather must be

"externally induced" by forces working with an altered consciousness and an awareness

"that the existing social order is *unjust* and *unnatural*." In other words, women must first

"be convinced of their innate right to equality, dignity, and justice" (Batliwala 1994:

132). Critical consciousness, for Batliwala, is therefore a prerequisite for building a mass movement that challenges and transforms the existing power relations in society.

Batliwala (1994) argues that, through empowerment, women gain access to new worlds of knowledge and can begin to make new, informed choices in both their personal and public lives. However, such radical changes, Batliwala argues, are not sustainable if limited to a few individual women. The empowerment process, she contends, must therefore organize women into collectives, "breaking out from individual isolation and creating a united forum through which women can challenge their subordination" (Batliwala 1994: 132). With the support of the collective and the activist agent, Batliwala (1994: 132) asserts, "women can re-examine their lives critically, recognize the structures and sources of power and subordination, discover their strengths, and initiate action." Batliwala, therefore, defines power as "control over material assets, intellectual resources, and ideology" (1994: 129) and empowerment as "the process of challenging existing power relations, and of gaining greater control over the sources of power" (1994: 130).

Batliwala (2007) laments, however, that over the past several decades, the term, "empowerment," has been "mainstreamed" in a manner that has all but robbed it of its original meaning, as well as its strategic value. As Batliwala (2007: 558) explains, while "empowerment" acquired a strong political meaning in the latter half of the twentieth century, as it was adopted by Black power, feminist, and other social movements engaged in struggles for more equitable, participatory, and democratic forms of social change and development, in the 1990s, it was converted from a collective to an individualistic process, and "skillfully co-opted by conservative and even reactionary political ideologies in pursuit of their agenda of divesting 'big government' (for which read: the welfare state) of its purported power and control by 'empowering' communities to look after their own affairs.'"

Sardenberg (2008) echoes these claims, in arguing that, despite efforts to promote women's empowerment throughout the world, little thinking has gone into depicting how power travels through individuals, groups, and institutions, and therefore toward linking gains at the institutional level with real changes in the everyday lives of women. Feminist thinking, she argues, lacks concerted analysis of the linkages and discontinuities between individual agency, collection action, and structural transformation, and how they operate in the process of women's empowerment and the eradication of patriarchal domination. This brings Sardenberg to a discussion of two competing forms of empowerment, which she terms "liberal empowerment" and "liberating empowerment." Liberal empowerment, Sardenberg (2008) argues, regards women's empowerment as an instrument for development priorities, be they eradicating poverty or building democracy. Consistent with liberal ideals, she explains, the focus is on individual growth, and is an approach that de-politicizes the process of empowerment by taking power out of the equation. *Liberating* empowerment, by contrast, addresses the unequal power relations between women and men as its central issue, and conceptualizes empowerment as the process by which women attain autonomy and self-determination, "as well as an instrument for the eradication of patriarchy, a means and an end in itself (Sardenberg 2008: 19). Such an approach, she explains, is consistent with a focus on women's organizing and collective action, though she clarifies that the importance of empowerment on a personal level should not be disregarded.

Sardenberg (2008) traces the origins of liberal empowerment to both classical liberalism and liberal feminism's claim for equality and equal opportunities for women. Sardenberg stresses, however, that because liberalism is not only associated with a political theory centered on notions of individual liberty, individual rights, and equal opportunity, but also with neoclassical economics, it produces views and policies that align with the demands of the market for structural adjustment, privatization, and the downsizing of the state. As Sardenberg (2008) argues, this approach ignores the structure of patriarchal dominance that underlines inequalities between women and men, as well as class, race, ethnicity and other social determinants responsible for the inequalities among women. In other words, rather than addressing the existing power structure, liberal empowerment merely addresses "the fact that women have not benefitted from it" (Kabeer 1994: 20).

Cornwall (2016: 342) argues that, while "empowerment" was once used to describe grassroots struggles to confront and transform unjust and unequal power relations, it has since become a term used by an "expansive discourse coalition of corporations, global non-governmental organizations, banks, philanthrocapitalists, and development donors." In the process, she argues, many insights from feminist conceptual work carried out in the 1980s and 1990s have been lost. She argues that "women's empowerment" came to be articulated in the 1980s and 1990s as a radical approach concerned with transforming power relations in favor of women's rights and greater equality between women and men. Conceptualized in this way, women's empowerment represented an unfolding process of changes in consciousness and collective power that would bring about structural change in favor of greater equality. Increasingly, however, she contends that empowerment is being used in a way that erases the need for structural change through a focus on enhancing the capacity of individuals to increase their human capital and elevate themselves out of their circumstances.

Radhakrishnan and Solari (2022) argue that this reconceptualization of women's empowerment from a collective to an individual endeavor did not happen by accident. Rather, they argue that this transformation was directly tied to the Cold War between the United States and the former Soviet Union, explaining that because "collective empowerment" was associated with the USSR and communism, the United States opposed it. They explain that, despite the fact that individualistic understandings of empowerment were incompatible with those emerging from feminist organizing around the world, "individual empowerment" achieved discursive dominance, in part, thanks to a shift in the women's empowerment debate from the United Nations to the World Bank, the rise of human capital theory (Becker 1964), and the collapse of the Soviet Union. According to Radhakrishnan and Solari (2022), through this process, women's "empowerment" became ubiquitous as a mode of discourse but became associated with enhancing the "untapped" potential (read: human capital) of women rather than addressing the structural barriers that limited their autonomy. As a result, they argue, the image of a new "empowered woman" emerged, which they describe as "a racialized figure who, through investing in herself, will lift her family and her country out of poverty without transforming social or economic structures." They stress that this reconceptualization of women's empowerment serves to bolster neoliberal capitalism to the detriment of women and marginalized groups while erasing decades of feminist grassroots and transnational organizing. They conclude, however, that by becoming aware of the history of women's empowerment, we can recover varied collectivist interpretations of empowerment that can help us imagine more equitable paths forward (Radhakrishnan and Solari 2022).

An examination of the women's sports literature reveals the influence of this reconceptualization on sports scholars' understandings of empowerment. Studies within this body of scholarship have increasingly conceptualized empowerment in individualized and symbolic terms with seemingly little thinking going into how women's embrace of physicality and athleticism might translate into collective action on behalf of women as a group, or into challenges to the social structures that shape the unequal power relations between men and women throughout society. Further, studies of women's empowerment in sport have consistently failed to show how women's participation in sport leads to the development of a critical consciousness, thereby calling the strength of this "empowerment" into question. In the following section, I examine a more recent trend in the women's sports literature—the application of McCaughey's (1997) "physical feminism" theory to studies of martial arts and combat sports (MACS)—to analyze the ways in which women's embrace of physical power through MACS has increasingly been conceptualized as a form of *physical* empowerment and liberation.

Physical Feminism and Martial Arts and Combat Sports (MACS)

Physical feminism is a branch of feminism that encourages women to embrace their physical power as a means of resisting rape culture and unlearning the social scripts that prescribe women's passivity, learned helplessness, and fear of violence (McCaughey 1997). McCaughey (1997) argues that the identification of violence with patriarchy by radical feminists has itself been a successful patriarchal regulatory method supporting the embodied oppression of women. By learning to *embrace* their capacity for violence, rather than rejecting it, McCaughey (1997) argues that women can unlearn the "rape scripts" that reinforce "the hegemonic belief that women need protection from bad men by good men" (Burke 2019: 502). As summarized by McCaughey (1997: 8),

> Women who take self-defense instruction, with whatever motivations and ideological perspectives, are offered an implicit or explicit critique of the ways in which gender is constructed in a culture of male privilege which rests on the abuse of women. What is usually taken for granted as a fact of nature—that a woman simply cannot physically challenge a man—is revealed as a social script which privileges men at the expense of women. The influence of gender ideologies on our bodily dispositions surfaces in self-defense instruction, where women gain the capacity for verbal and physical aggression. Gender ideology is thus not simply a matter of the mind; it includes embodied social values. Self-defense offers the possibility of a critical consciousness of gender's influence on what we see as male and female bodies. As such, it is a "final frontier" of feminist consciousness-raising—an effort that has traditionally focused on the mind, not the body, as the recipient of ideology.

For McCaughey (1997), women's self-defense training represents a form of feminist consciousness-raising, as it allows women participants to discover their capacity to resist male domination and, in the process, become more aware of the socially constructed nature of male privilege. Part of this process, McCaughey (1997) argues, is the "unlearning" of femininity. McCaughey cites MacKinnon (1987: 54) in stating that, "femininity…is how [women] come to want male dominance, which most emphatically is not in [their] interest" (McCaughey 1997: 37). Because women are rewarded for cultivating physical and behavioral difference from men, McCaughey (1997) argues, women are coerced into embodying femininity in ways that render gender inequality "sexy" and desirable. Self-defense courses, she argues, make visible women's embodiment of "feminine helplessness" (McCaughey 1997: 59) and, thus, allow women to unlearn it. As summarized by McCaughey (1997: 90), "What feminists talk about interrupting—femininity—self defensers practice interrupting: They enact the deconstruction of femininity. In the process, self-defense enables women to internalize a different kind of bodily knowledge. As such, self-defense is feminism in the flesh." Through this process, McCaughey (1998) argues, women learn a new bodily comportment that not only increases their ability to defend themselves against male violence but also proves highly consequential for many areas of their lives.

Building on McCaughey's (1997) physical feminism theory, Roth and Basow (2004) proposed a "physically based feminist liberation strategy." They cite Castelnuovo and Guthrie's (1994: 13) call for feminists to advance a liberatory strategy in which women are "empowered physically, not just mentally" and identify sports as a potential site through which women might enact such a strategy. They argue that women who participate in contact sports and self-defense training are likely to gain confidence and enjoyment from their participation. They further assert that such women gain a sense of security against rape that is unavailable to most women. They argue that such benefits hold potential to extend to women as a group, as they would allow *all* women the ability to escape the "rape mystique" that limits women's autonomy by keeping them fearful and forcing them to constrict their lives. As such, women's development of physical power offers potential not just to enhance individual women's ability to prevent rape but also to serve as a radical challenge to the sexual scripts that dictate female passivity and vulnerability and male dominance and aggression.

Noel (2009) advocates for physical feminism through martial arts training. According to Noel (2009), the benefits of martial arts and self-defense training can include physical and psychological empowerment for women. She argues that such empowerment could include reduced fear of crime, increased confidence, increased self-efficacy, increased sense of control to prevent an attack, increased ability to stop an attempted rape, reduced feelings of vulnerability, positive therapeutic outcomes for sexual assault survivors, and an increase in women's perceptions of their strength compared to men. She argues that martial arts is an avenue through which women can challenge societal messages that position women as weak and vulnerable to violence and therefore represents an appropriate venue for the development of physical feminism.

Channon and Phipps (2017) also advocate for physical feminism through martial arts and combat sports (MACS). They argue that women's movement into the "masculine" world of MACS has the potential to pose "particularly dramatic challenges to wider social discourses of male superiority, owing to the way in which female fighting ability and the combat-ready female body destabalise patriarchal gender norms and women's concurrent symbolic subordination to men" (Channon and Phipps 2017: 25). They point out, however, that research has documented a tendency for MACS practitioners to resist or counteract the gender-subversive potential of women's MACS

practice through modes of practice and/or representation which "reify, rather than

challenge, hierarchal gender relations" (Channon and Phipps 2017: 25). How MACS

practitioners "do" gender (West and Zimmerman 1987), therefore, is of particular

importance in mediating the potentially transformative consequences of women's

integration into an otherwise ostensibly "masculine" cultural sphere.

Channon and Phipps (2017) do not agree, however, with McCaughey's (1997)

contention that a physical feminism necessitates the "unlearning" of femininity. Rather,

they argue that women MACS practitioners construct "alternative femininities"

(Schippers 2002; Carlson 2010; Finley 2010) that are "intelligible as feminine but work

against the maintenance of male hegemony" (Channon and Phipps 2017: 27). Such

femininities, they argue, overtly signify both "woman" and "power," and, as such,

represent a genuine alternative to patriarchal conceptions of femininity. As summarized

by Channon and Phipps (2017: 32),

> Taken together, the findings of our studies reveal how specific articulations of
> femininity are purposefully chosen by women participating in MACS, and
> deliberately enacted/enjoyed in accordance with their own self-authorised sense
> of identity. Many of our interviewees used language that framed femininity as
> something desirable and intrinsically valuable; they didn't want to have to "go
> without", "lose," or "sacrifice" to become a fighter. And, with this in mind, they
> articulated specific ways in which femininity could be happily accommodated
> with the demands of MACS participation. Critical of instances wherein certain
> aspects of femininity could obstruct training, or give a poor impression of women
> fighters to others, it was clear that feminine behaviours needed to be carefully
> negotiated in order to signify both "woman" and "fighter." Furthermore, it was
> broadly noted that such successful gender performances bore value—they could
> help develop wider (female) participation in MACS; they might confer some
> competitive advantages in the ring; most of all they carried the potential to
> challenge sexist beliefs about women's capabilities and destablise the hierarchical
> constructs through which sexual difference is commonly imagined.

Channon and Phipps (2017) conclude, therefore, that scholarly work on women's MACS and gender performances should attend more closely to the manner in which the performance of alterative femininities by women fighters might work against gender hierarchies.

Maor (2019) also advocates for MACS as a site of physical feminism. She argues that martial arts is particularly well-suited for studying how physical activity can change gender hierarchies. By performing movements and actions that are strongly associated with masculinity, she argues that women confront the normative gendered regimes of restricting movement and limiting physical potential through their participation in martial arts. Like Channon and Phipps (2017), Maor argues that physical feminism does not necessitate abandoning performances of femininity. Rather, she argues that scholars should attend to the potentially subversive value of "hybrid" femininities. She states:

> When applied to the study of gender and sport, the hypothesized negative relationship between empowerment and performances of femininity leads scholars to view performances of femininity as blocking or countering the subversive potential of women's involvement in "masculine" sports. Thus, female athletes who exhibit performances of femininity outside of sport settings are judged to be compensating for their nonconformity or "selling out" to patriarchy (Follo 2012; Channon and Phipps 2016). These authors fail to recognize the potentially subversive value of performances of femininity in different contexts: for instance, when combined with performances of masculinity (e.g., queer or hybrid femininities), or when employed strategically.

Maor (2019) warns, however, that, as long as women are a minority in most martial arts groups, it is likely that women practitioners may come to view themselves as "exceptional women," or "honorary men," who are "thereby dismissed from troubling symbolic constructions of male superiority" (Channon and Phipps 2017: 27: Maor 2019:

37). She argues, therefore, that empowerment through learning to fight is not self-evident but is contingent on specific circumstances.

Burke (2019) offers a critique of scholars' use of physical feminism theory (McCaughey 1997) in studies of "masculine" sports. While recognizing that women's participation in these sports offers potential to be "individually empowering," he is not convinced that this participation can lead to the broader feminist political transformations that McCaughey (1997) theorizes. He stresses that McCaughey's (1997) physical feminism theory contains two elements: a personally empowering change in the women who engage in self-defense classes, and "a specific political-epistemological challenge to the 'rape culture' narrative of the broader society" (Burke 2019: 503). While women who participate in "masculine" sports may experience both physical and psychological benefits, he explains, their effects are likely to be less radical. As explained by Burke (2019: 503), "In contrast to the scripts learnt by self-defenders, women who enter female competitions in previously 'masculine sports,' where they perform against other women, may learn a new script, but it is not a script that challenges patriarchal power. If anything, it reinforces the hegemony." Burke (2019: 503) contends, therefore, that women's participation in "masculine sports" may be "simultaneously *both* empowering and oppressive." In light of these considerations, Burke (2019) proposes three commitments that should be made within women's sports to achieve feminist epistemological-political gains:

1. The importance of consciousness-raising
2. The need for collective and women-centered organizations

3. A radical challenge to the broader patriarchal discourse, including its

   contextualization in neoliberal capitalism.

Taken together, these studies suggest that, while MACS may be a site where the presumed negative relationship between femininity and physical power is challenged, the extent to which this challenge translates into broader feminist transformations is unclear. Furthermore, these studies suggest that the "empowerment" potential of MACS participation is mediated by other cultural and/or environmental factors that may well negate its effects. How this process is currently unfolding within the sport of WMMA, however, remains an open empirical question. In the following section, I examine the small but growing literature on WMMA and discuss its potential as a site of physical feminism and women's empowerment.

Women's Mixed Martial Arts (WMMA)

Channon and Jennings (2013) provide, perhaps, the first sociological account of women's participation in MMA. Drawing from interviews with WMMA athletes, as well as women athletes from Brazilian jiu-jitsu, muay Thai, and various other combat sports, they argue that the mixed-sex training environment of MMA provides a "lived-out 'undoing' of gender" (Channon and Jennings 2013: 15). While recognizing that this is not a uniform experience for all MMA and MACS participants, they argue that such training is consistent with the goals of physical feminism (McCaughey 1997) and state that their findings indicate that "the potential to subversively 'undo' gender exists within mixed-sex martial arts, as within other integrated physical cultures" (Channon and Jennings 2013: 15).

Channon (2014) extends this analysis and further advocates the "undoing" of gender through mixed-sex MACS training. He includes testimonies from women MMA practitioners and argues that, following their experiences of integrated training, the participants in his study rejected patriarchal gender ideals. He concludes, however, that further research is needed to conform or refute his findings.

Mierzwinski, Velija, and Malcolm (2014) argue that women are motivated to participate in MMA by a gendered "quest for excitement" and that such women "directly experience elements of empowerment" (Mierzinwsinki, Velija, and Malcolm 2014: 75). They argue that, through the development and demonstration of physical strength (and technique), women MMA participants are able to "challenge a traditional and fundamental pillar of male dominance" (Mierzwinski, Velija, and Malcolm 2014: 75). They note, however, that MMA is a space where women are routinely marginalized, but that "the sense of empowerment female mixed martial arts experience should not be underestimated" (Mierzwinski, Velija, and Malcolm 2014: 81). They contend, therefore, that the growth of women's involvement in MMA reflects "a movement toward greater equality" (Mierzwinski, Velija, and Malcolm 2014: 81).

Weaving (2014) argues that women's participation in MMA challenges traditional stereotypes of female physical passivity and attempts at physical invisibility. She contends that MMA provides women with opportunities to realize lived bodily experiences and challenge outdated claims of women's bodily capabilities. She recognizes, however, that the culture of MMA remains male-dominated and sexist. She also recognizes that, despite the potential for transgressive lived bodily experiences for women fighters, women are still persistently portrayed as sex objects in MMA discourse. Such framing, she contends, "impacts the lived body experiences that are possible for female UFC participants, and moreover, even the types of women that have participation made available to them" (Weaving 2014: 135).

McClearen (2015) examines the treatment of transwoman fighter, Fallon Fox, by MMA athletes and media. She shows how the reactions to Fox's coming out as transgender were shaped by interlocking discourses of sexism and cissexism. She details, for instance, how former UFC athlete, Matt Mitrione, referred to Fox as a "lying, sick, sociopathic, disgusting freak" in an interview with MMA journalist, Ariel Helwani, and how UFC commentator, Joe Rogan, asserted that allowing Fox to fight other women would lead to an abuse of power by other "crazy" transwomen athletes who want to "beat the fuck out of chicks" (McClearen 2021: 80). She also details the ways in which cis women MMA athletes responded to Fox coming out as transgender. She includes statements from WMMA athletes such as Miesha Tate, who clarified that she would only compete against Fox if the medical community could prove Fox was "100% female" (McClearen 2015: 82), and Peggy Morgan, who stated that, "As an athlete and a woman, I am frustrated by the way the situation has played out and by the fact that many people seem more concerned with preserving Fallon's feelings than with protecting the physical safety of me and the other female competitors in the tournament" (McClearen 2015: 82). She argues that the discourse surrounding Fox's participation in WMMA reaffirms a "patriarchal, cisgender, cissexual system of power by exaggerating 'biologically' sanctioned male physical dominance and 'innate' female physical lack" (McClearen 2015: 74).

Jennings (2015) provides a critique of the UFC's promotion of their women athletes through an analysis of *The Ultimate Fighter Season 20's* promotional campaign, "Beauty and Strength." She details the ways in which the promotional video for *TUF 20* focused on the fighters' appearances, rather than their skills, and marketed the athletes in sexist dichotomies such as "jaw-dropping" and "jaw-breaking," and "easy on the eyes" and "hard on the face." She argues that the video, in effect, conveys the message that, while these women may be fighters, they are "women, beautiful women, first" and that, for WMMA athletes, their first function is to serve the male gaze (Jennings 2015: 73).

Quinney (2015) analyzes the framing of women UFC fighters on Twitter over a four-year period. Through an intersectional feminist analysis, she examines how Twitter users frame WMMA athletes' bodies in relation to gender, race, class, and sexuality. She argues that there is an imbalance in attention paid to white, cis gender, and straight women fighters, and that this imbalance communicates contradictory messages about feminism, WMMA athletes' bodies, and the UFC. She concludes, therefore, that such discourse amounts to "faux feminism," as WMMA athletes are framed in "static and narrow ways" (Quinney 2015: 58).

Jakubowska, Channon, and Matthews (2016) analyze Polish media coverage of Polish WMMA athlete and former UFC champion, Joanna Jedrzejczyk. They argue that their findings reveal "a relatively de-gendered, widely celebratory account, primarily framed by nationalistic discourse"—findings they attribute to "both the particularities of the sport of mixed martial arts as well as the historic nature of Jedrzejczyk's success" (Jakubowska, Channon, and Matthews 2016: 410). While careful not to overly attribute the uniqueness of Jedrzejczyk's coverage to the "exceptional" nature of MMA, the authors nevertheless argue that there are few other cultural spaces within which such dramatically visceral examples of skill, tenacity, and embodied power can be observed with such regularity. They argue, therefore, that WMMA athletes "stand to dramatically challenge dominant gender norms when their feats are properly recognized," and that their data add to "a growing body of knowledge that recognizes the potential that female fighters hold to challenge, subvert, and re-write traditional gendered logic" (Jakubowska, Channon, and Matthews 2016: 425).

Chisholm, Weaving, and Bischoping (2016) examine the gendered significance of WMMA through an analysis of MMA media and internet user comments. They discern three discourses which they argued feature prominent in WMMA: (1) a celebratory late twentieth and early twenty-first century Girl Power discourse, (2) a longer-standing discourse in which Amazons of Greek myth are the forebears of women in MMA, and (3) a discourse in which the UFC and other MMA companies' practices, and women's participation in them, are understood as neoliberal risk performers. They argue that, while individual WMMA athletes may experience their subjectivities as empowering, when considering MMA practices, their popular representations, and their reception, "the fanfares about Girl Power quickly strike what, for feminists, are sour notes" (Chisholm, Weaving, and Bischoping 2016: 282). They conclude:

> Across each of the discourses we encountered, we did not find women's UFC
> performances to be signaling political change. While each in its own way

celebrates women's capacities as cage fighters, they all neutralize criticism of the more common, historical reality of women's experience of violence by men. They do not, as such, invite critical inquiry into the gender systems that deny power to women *as a group*. Our findings indicate that despite the circulation of alternative discourses that appear to signal gender transgression, the inclusion and participation of women in MMA has not challenged gender norms. Regardless of women's relative success in this male-dominated sport, it remains a difficult site in which to produce meaningful shifts in gendered relations of power. Such findings raise the question of the real political influence of women's inclusion into the world(s) of men (Chisholm, Weaving, and Bischoping 2016: 282).

McClearen (2018) provides a discourse analysis of UFC media. She shows how discourses of postfeminism, popular feminism, antifeminism, misogyny, and racism all circulate under the umbrella of UFC media. She argues that the UFC's decision to promote "empowered" female fighters was an attempt to capitalize on the "cultural resonance" of women's empowerment by promoting their women's divisions as a revolution for women and women's sports (McClearen 2018: 45). She stresses, however, that the UFC's embrace of women's empowerment is "ideologically uneven" (McClearen 2018: 45) and largely excludes Black women and other women of color. She argues, therefore, that, while discourses of women and girls' physical empowerment in UFC media present a challenge to the construction of white femininity, "in the end, the strong white feminine body becomes a vehicle for supporting neoliberal brand culture and maintaining hegemonic femininity and whiteness" (McClearen 2018: 60).

Channon et al. (2018) examine the sexualization of women athletes in MMA, and how WMMA athletes' sexualized bodies are positioned relative to discourses of gender, neoliberal selfhood, and athlete commodification. They discuss the sexualization of WMMA athletes by MMA media, as well as how WMMA athletes' acts of self-sexualization are framed as acts of "empowerment." As stated by Channon et al. (2018: 387),

> This discursive conflation of choice, freedom, and autonomy with public nudity risks reducing women's "empowerment" to a simple matter of going along with existing patterns of commodified, heteronormative sexual performance, or not— rather than speaking up against the structural inequalities that these practices help to reinforce.

Channon et al. (2018) also discuss the prevalence of anti-feminist discourse in WMMA. As an example, they cite an Instagram post by former UFC athlete, Bec Rawlings, which features a photo of her nude body holding a sign that reads, "Fuck feminism. I believe in human rights…for all!!!" Connecting Rawlings' erroneous statement about feminism to the influences of neoliberalism and postfeminism, they explain,

> This statement exemplifies the ideological work performed by postfeminist discourse; feminism is positioned as a coercive practice which constructs women as "weak victims," while the sexualized, powerful, and "free" body of the WMMA fighter becomes a symbol of women's agency in a world which no longer needs feminist interventions (Channon et al. 2018: 387).

They conclude that, while the sexualization of women fighters may capture the attention of some fans and sponsors in the short term, it could risk undermining their credibility as athletes, as well as reproducing inequalities between fighters and thus harming the sport as a whole.

McClearen (2021) provides an illuminating look into the exploitative business practices of the UFC, and how these practices shape the experiences of women fighters who compete for the promotion. She argues that the UFC's business practices force WMMA athletes to devote countless hours to online self-promotion while allowing the

UFC to remain the primary benefactor of these athletes' labor. She stresses that in order for UFC athletes to improve their situation, collective action is needed. She notes however that, in order for fighters to successfully organize, they will need to overcome the organizational conditions that prevent them from joining unionization efforts, such as fear of retaliation, lack of support from UFC stars, individualism, and isolation. McClearen (2021: 160) concludes, therefore, that "the only way for…advocacy efforts to take flight is to reconfigure the perception of fighters as being an island unto themselves and instead leverage their political visibility into a collective front fighting for all."

Taken together, these studies suggest that, while the sport of WMMA holds potential to serve as a site through which women athletes challenge patriarchal constructions of gender and influence feminist change, the extent to which this is currently being realized is unclear. The extent to which WMMA is serving as a space of empowerment is, therefore, also unclear. In the following section, I outline the present study which addresses these knowledge gaps through an ethnographic study of WMMA.

THE PRESENT STUDY

The present study is a critical ethnography of women's mixed martial arts (WMMA). Drawing from multiple qualitative methods, including participant observation, semi-structured interviews, and content analysis, this study aims to address the gaps in the women's sports and empowerment literatures and provide insight for how MACS can fulfill their potential as sites of empowerment and liberation. Examining WMMA through an "insider-outsider" perspective (Dwyer and Buckle 2009) and intersectional feminist lens, my study offers the most thorough sociological account of WMMA to date and provides a critical analysis of its potential as a site of women's empowerment.

Dissertation Overview

In this chapter, I have attempted to outline a brief history of WMMA, as well as the rising political and cultural significance of this new sport, before situating it in broader discussions of gender, feminism, and women's empowerment. I have shown how media and scholars alike have consistently framed WMMA as a space of empowerment, and how MMA's culture of far-right politics, white supremacy, and hypermasculinity stands in stark contrast to this framing. I have also provided a summary of the small (but growing) literature on WMMA and highlighted the gaps in this body of research.

In Chapter 2, I detail my research methodology and sample, as well as my positionality. As a former MMA athlete, myself, I discuss my perspective as an "insider-outsider" (Dwyer and Buckle 2009), as well as my motivations for studying women MMA athletes. I describe how my interest in researching these athletes was motivated by nearly fifteen years of experience in the sport of MMA, where I have participated as both an athlete and a coach. Routinely seeing depictions of WMMA as "transgressive" and "empowering," following women's entrée into the UFC, I describe how I found myself unable to reconcile these accounts with what I had experienced as an overtly conservative and misogynistic field. I explain how I, therefore, set out to understand how women's participation in MMA impacted their personal lives and to what extent we should characterize this new sport as "empowering."

In Chapter 3, I offer a robust sociological description of WMMA culture, politics, and subjecthood. I highlight themes that emerged from my participant-observation in an MMA academy in Southern California, as well as through my content analysis of MMA media. I show how MMA culture provides ideological support for the reproduction of neoliberal capitalist values through its emphasis on self-discipline, -surveillance, and -cultivation, as well as its alignment with conservative and far-right politics. I also introduce an original concept, which I term, "the breaking barriers paradox," to show how women's achievements in MMA (and elsewhere) are framed as both a source of women's empowerment and a celebration of women's liberation.

In Chapter 4, I discuss the doing and selling of gender in WMMA and introduce two original concepts, which I term, "the female-athlete commodity" and "doing both." Utilizing these concepts, I show how WMMA athletes "do" gender (West and Zimmerman 1987) in ways that allow them to benefit from their association with both hegemonic masculinity and (white) heterofemininity, and how this comes at the expense of queer women and women of color. I explicate this strategy through a critical analysis of a social media "empowerment" campaign in which WMMA athletes participated under the hashtag, #GetYouAGirlThatCanDoBoth. I also include testimonies from my interviews with WMMA athletes.

In Chapter 5, I describe how WMMA athletes "do" heterosexuality (West and Zimmerman 1987; Schilt and Westbrook 2009) in their intimate relationships. I find that heterosexual WMMA athletes accomplish heterofemininity in their intimate relationships through three specific actions: 1.) partnering with men who are physically larger than them, 2.) partnering with men who are physically stronger and/or more powerful than them, and 3.) adhering to heteropatriarchal scripts. I argue, therefore, that women's participation in MMA does not lead to greater power in their intimate relationships. I conclude with a discussion of the ways in which these patterns may contribute to the epidemic of intimate partner violence (IPV) within the MMA community.

In Chapter 6, I call for a rethinking of women's empowerment in sport. I describe the ways in which "breaking barriers" discourse obscures women's understandings of empowerment and hinders their ability to understand their own oppression. I discuss the limitations of physical feminism (McCaughey 1997) in WMMA and offer suggestions for how martial arts and combat sports (MACS) can fulfill their liberatory potential. I also discuss the ways in which "breaking barriers" discourse frames women's participation in other arenas. Finally, I call for a reconceptualization of empowerment that centers intersectional concerns with capitalism, white supremacy, and heteropatriarchy.

CHAPTER II: ENTERING THE CAGE: RESEARCHING WOMEN'S MIXED MARTIAL ARTS

There are myriad ways through which one could choose to study women's mixed

martial arts. The literature on WMMA includes excellent examples of what can be gained

through discourse analysis (Channon et al. 2018; Chisholm, Weaving, and Bischoping

2016; McClearen 2015; McClearen 2018; Quinney 2015; Quinney 2016; Sailors and

Weaving 2017; Salvini and Marchi Júnior 2016), content analysis (Jennings 2015), and

media and cultural studies (Jakubowska, Channon, and Matthews 2016; McClearen 2021;

Weaving 2014), as well as through semistructured interviews (Channon 2014; Channon

and Jennings 2013; Mierzwinski, Velija, and Malcolm 2014). Using these research

methodologies, scholars have informed us about the various discourses that pervade

WMMA culture (e.g., Jennings 2015; McClearen 2015; McClearen 2018; Weaving 2014;

Quinney 2015), the exploitative business practices of the UFC (McClearen 2021), and the

potential for WMMA to serve as a site of feminist social change (Channon 2014;

Channon and Jennings 2013; Jakubowska, Channon, and Matthews 2016; Mierzwinski,

Velija, and Malcolm 2014; Quinney 2015; Weaving 2014).

What has often been missing from these studies, however, is a "thick" description

(Geertz 1973) of WMMA athletes' social worlds, as well as an experientially-informed

understanding of these athletes' subjectivities. Scholars researching WMMA have

typically included MMA "outsiders" (e.g., Quinney 2015; Mierzwinski, Velija, and

Malcolm 2014) or researchers who began studying WMMA in their early development as

martial arts hobbyists (e.g., Channon 2014; Channon and Jennings 2013; Channon and

Matthews 2016). While these scholars' perspectives are important, there is much to be gained from an experientially-informed "insider" perspective of the unique subculture of MMA.

In this chapter, I offer a detailed description of my research methodology and sample, and discuss my perspective as an "insider-outsider" (Dwyer and Buckle 2009) in the world of WMMA. I explain how I initially became interested in studying WMMA athletes and how my years of experience in men's MMA allowed me to gain access to a group of elite WMMA athletes to whom I might not otherwise have been able to gain access. I explain how my expertise in MMA led to my becoming the head coach of one of these athletes, and how this experience afforded me the unique opportunity to travel to Southeast Asia three times throughout the course of this project to coach her in MMA competition. I also discuss the lessons my dissertation offers for understanding the benefits of qualitative research, as well as for understanding the unique role of history in shaping ethnographic studies. Finally, I discuss the linkages between feminist theory and praxis, and how feminist and profeminist scholars can use their work to influence feminist social change.

RESEARCH DESIGN AND METHODS

The present study is a critical ethnography of women's mixed martial arts. It draws from multiple qualitative methods, including more than four years of ethnographic research on the sport of WMMA and 40 semistructured interviews with professional WMMA athletes. This multi-site, multi-year ethnography involved participant observation at an MMA academy that boasts one of the largest professional WMMA teams in the United States, conversational interviews with MMA athletes and trainers, content analysis of MMA media, and the rare opportunity to serve as head coach to an elite WMMA athlete while conducting my research. These multiple qualitative methods allowed me to construct the most thorough sociological description of WMMA to date and afforded me a perspective that is currently lacking in the WMMA literature.

Semistructured Interviews

The 40 semistructured interviews all took place in-person, were digitally audio-recorded, and transcribed verbatim. The interviews lasted between one to two hours and covered a wide range of topics, including the athletes' conceptions of empowerment, their beliefs about gender, their experiences of gendered harassment, and their relationships with intimate partners. Conducting the interviews in person provided me the ability to not only see and interpret how the interviewees were responding in real time but also gain a greater sense of these athletes' daily lives. Interviewing numerous athletes in their homes, for example, allowed me to observe them as they cared for their children or loved ones and provided me additional insight into these athletes' daily routines. I also interviewed several of the athletes at their workplaces and training academies which also provided me insight into these athletes' social networks.

Participant Observation

In addition to conducting 40 semistructured interviews, I also conducted participant observation at an MMA academy in Southern California. My entrée into the academy was facilitated by several of my interview participants. Initially, I entered the academy to participate in a single Brazilian Jiu-Jitsu class in hopes of recruiting additional research participants for my semistructured interviews. Upon entering the academy and being introduced to several of the team's athletes and coaches, I decided it would be beneficial to spend more time training alongside the athletes to get a better sense of my interview participants' social worlds. Eventually, I realized the academy could serve as an excellent site for ethnographic study and sought permission from the owner to conduct further research. Upon receiving permission, I began the process of making weekly trips to the academy to train alongside the athletes, conduct conversational interviews, attend social gatherings, and build relationships.

My time at the academy afforded me unprecedented insight into the lives of professional WMMA athletes. Throughout my time there, I was introduced to dozens of WMMA athletes, as well as coaches, managers, sponsors, parents, friends, partners, and peers. The athletes' statuses ranged from professional world champions to MMA novices at the beginning of their amateur careers. To document my time at the academy, I utilized hand-written notes, as well as digital notes, audio recordings, video recordings, photographs, and voice memos. I utilized these tools not only to capture what I had observed but also reflect on my own experiences. I would, for example, often record voice memos on my phone while driving home from the academy to reflect on the day's events. This provided an opportunity to not only articulate what I was experiencing in real-time but also reflect on how my experiences and impressions changed over time.

In addition to conducting participation observation at the MMA academy, I also attended several of the athletes' fights and media appearances. These fights ranged from amateur bouts against other athletes at the early stages of their careers to world championship title fights against some of the sport's most accomplished fighters. I became acquainted with the routine of appearing with the athletes for radio interviews, TV interviews, and internet interviews, as well as for photoshoots, medical evaluations, and various other pre-fight obligations. I followed the athletes as they dealt with injuries, cut weight before competition, and ultimately experienced "the thrill of victory and the agony of defeat." These experiences provided me invaluable insight not only into the mundane, day-to-day events that comprise much of WMMA athletes' daily lives, but also the unique moments WMMA athletes experience in their exhilarating (although often fleeting) encounters with triumph, celebrity, and fame.

Coaching

Throughout the course of this project, I unexpectedly became the head coach of a WMMA athlete, myself. I initially became acquainted with this athlete through one of my semistructured interviews. After our interview, I offered the athlete a free personal MMA training session, as I did with each of the athletes I interviewed. This session led to the athlete purchasing several more sessions with me and eventually approaching me about becoming her head coach—an offer I cautiously accepted. As this athlete's coach, my duties included training and sparring alongside her on a daily basis; overseeing her progress both in person and through recorded sparring sessions; securing additional training resources for her such as dieticians, strength and conditioning coaches, psychological coaches, and training partners; providing guidance on which bouts to accept, when to accept them, and how to prepare for them; and cornering her in MMA competition. Because this athlete was signed to a major MMA promotion based in Southeast Asia, I was afforded the rare opportunity to travel with her to Asia and coach her in one of the sport's biggest promotions. I coached her to two professional wins and one professional loss, competing twice in Kuala Lumpur, Malaysia, and once in Singapore. Through these experiences, I became intimately familiar with the business of MMA, and I was afforded the opportunity to interact with commentators, matchmakers, public relations representatives, social media strategists, referees, medical officials, and many other professionals working in the MMA industry. Serving as this athlete's head coach afforded me the unique opportunity to further embed myself in the world of WMMA and follow this athlete for several years as she progressed through her MMA career. This experience, alongside my other qualitative methods, allowed me to paint a more complete picture of the world of WMMA and offer a more holistic account of WMMA athletes' social worlds.

SAMPLE AND RECRUITMENT

To recruit athletes for my study, I began by searching on the MMA athlete database, Tapology.com, which allowed me to search for fighters by gender, weight class, and region. Once I had compiled a list of fighters in my region, I searched for these athletes on social media and began contacting them about participating in my study. Additional participants were recruited through snowball sampling methods until saturation was achieved. The use of social media proved to be an effective strategy, as it allowed me to showcase my MMA experience and credentials, and establish trust with the athletes before conducting my interviews. Once meeting the athletes in person, my "cauliflower ears" were also easily spotted and served to further demonstrate my commitment to the sport of MMA. Such visible, embodied markers of membership within the community aided in my ability to establish trust and rapport and became common icebreakers for the women in this study.

Occasionally, however, the athletes' social media profiles would be managed by someone else (usually their husband), which sometimes proved to be a barrier to accessing the athlete. On one occasion, for example, an athlete's husband informed me that the athlete would not participate in an interview unless he could approve the questions beforehand and be present for the interview. When I informed him that he would not be allowed to sit in on the interview, he quickly declined.

In recruiting athletes for my study, I employed a theoretical sampling strategy (Coyne 1997) to ensure that I achieved as diverse of a sample as possible. I made strong efforts to recruit Black WMMA athletes in particular, as Black women are currently underrepresented in the sociology of sport literature (Bruening 2005). This proved difficult, however, as Black women are also underrepresented in WMMA. Still, I managed to achieve a diverse sample, including 22 women of color (55% of my sample) and 9 LGBTQ+ women (22.5% of my sample).

The athletes in my study were all active or retired professional MMA fighters with at least one fight on their professional records. Their ages ranged from 20- to 53-years-old with all but two of the athletes being between the ages of 20 and 40. The athletes' sexual identities included straight/heterosexual (77.5%), lesbian/homosexual (15%), bisexual (2.5%), and unlabeled (5%). Their racial identities included white (45%), Black (5%), Hispanic/Latina (17.5%), Asian (12.5%), Native Hawaiian (7.5%), and mixed (12.5%). Their education levels included high school diploma or general education diploma (25%), some college (25%), 2-year college degree (12.5%), 4-year college

degree (30%), and graduate school degree (7.5%). All of the athletes' names have been

changed to maintain their privacy and anonymity.

DATA ANALYSIS

After transcribing each of my semistructured interviews and organizing my

ethnographic materials, I used the qualitative data analysis software, ATLAS.ti, to

conduct my analysis. Utilizing an abductive analysis strategy, I merged deductive

theoretical insights with inductive analysis techniques in a "continuous process of

conjecturing" about my data (Tavory and Timmermans 2014; Timmermans and Tavory

2012: 172). Timmermans and Tavory (2012) argue that, despite the widespread

popularity and circulation of grounded theory (Glaser and Strauss 1967), scant theoretical

innovations have emerged from studies adopting this approach. Abductive analysis is,

therefore, a qualitative analysis approach aimed at theory construction (Timmermans and

Tavory 2012).

Abductive analysis rests on the cultivation of anomalous and/or surprising

empirical findings against a backdrop of multiple existing sociological theories and

through systematic methodological analysis (Timmermans and Tavory 2012). As

opposed to both grounded theory (Glaser and Strauss 1967) and the extended case

method (Burawoy 1998), abductive analysis prescribes that the researcher be neither a

"theoretical atheist" nor an "avowed monotheist" but rather an "informed theoretical

agnostic" (Timmermans and Tavory 2012: 169). While the logic of deduction prescribes

that the researcher begins with a rule and proceeds through a case to arrive at an observed result, and the logic of induction prescribes that the researcher begins with a collection of given cases and proceeds by examining their implied results to develop and an inference that some universal rule is operate, the logic of abduction prescribes that the researcher begins with consequences and then construct reasons (Timmermans and Tavory 2012). As explained by Timmermans and Tavory (2012: 171), "The surprising fact C is observed. But if A were true, C would be a matter of course. Hence, there is reason to suspect that A is true." I, therefore, began my analysis by focusing on anomalous and/or surprising results before engaging in a "dialectic of cultivated theoretical sensitivity and methodological heuristics" (Timmermans and Tavory 2012: 180).

Alongside my abductive analysis, I used flexible coding (Deterding and Waters 2021). I began by indexing transcripts with broad codes that connected to the concepts I originally sought to explore, such as "empowerment" and "femininity." From there, I applied more specific codes, such as "personal responsibility" and "natural sexual difference." Through this process, several distinct findings emerged, including the contradictory subjecthood of WMMA athletes, the unique commodification of gender in MMA, and the paradoxical effects of women's participation in MMA. Blending my abductive analysis with this flexible coding strategy, I was able to generate new theoretical insights into the unique subjecthood of WMMA athletes and offer a theoretically-informed assessment of WMMA's potential as a site of women's empowerment.

THEORETICAL FRAMEWORK

While an abductive analysis strategy was chosen for the purpose of theory construction, there were nevertheless several existing theories that guided my analysis and the interpretation of my data. These theories included neoliberalism (Harvey 2007), postfeminism (Gill 2007), "doing gender" theory (West and Zimmerman 1987), and intersectional feminist theory (Collins 2002; Combahee River Collective 1974; Crenshaw 1991). Utilizing these theories together allowed me to situate women's participation in MMA within a framework of social, political, and economic theory and analyze WMMA athletes' experiences through a distinctly sociological lens. In the following section, I detail my understanding of these theories and their relationship to WMMA and women's empowerment.

Neoliberalism

I understand neoliberalism as a political, economic, and social theory that proposes that human well-being can be best advanced by liberating individual entrepreneurial freedoms within an institutional framework characterized by strong private property rights, free markets, and free trade (Harvey 2007). While it initially rose to prominence in the late 1970s under Thatcher's premiership in the UK and throughout the 1980s under the Reagan administration in the US, since that point, it has come to dominate not just political and economic policy in the United States, but, increasingly, human rationality and subjecthood throughout the world (Harvey 2007). As explained by Harvey (2007: 3), "Neoliberalism has, in short, become hegemonic as a mode of discourse. It has pervasive effects on ways of thought to the point where it has become incorporated into the common-sense way many of us interpret, live in, and understand the world." Among its key tenets as a guiding principle for human action is its emphasis on individualism and personal responsibility over collective action and social welfare, perhaps, best captured by Thatcher's (1987) declaration that there is "no such thing" as society—only individual men and women.

Perhaps nowhere has the insidiousness of neoliberalism been more detrimental than within the project of women's empowerment (Gill and Scharff 2013). Indeed, much has been written about the connections between neoliberalism, feminism, and postfeminism, and the contradictory messages of which young women are the primary targets (e.g., Gill and Scharff 2013; McRobbie 2004; Rottenberg 2018). Among the central critiques of neoliberalism within the politics of women's empowerment has been its obfuscation of structural inequities that privilege white, affluent, heterosexual women at the expense of working-class women and women of color who bear the brunt of persistent inequities (hooks 2013; Rottenberg 2018, see Sandberg 2013, Slaughter 2012).

Postfeminism

Alongside neoliberalism, postfeminism has increasingly become an object of feminist cultural critique over the last decade (Gill 2016). The term originally rose to prominence in the 1990s as a way of understanding the paradoxes and contradictions in media representations of women and has since come to be used as a term for capturing the false sense that women are living in a post-sexist world, that any remaining inequities are the result of natural differences and/or of women's own choices, and, therefore, that feminism is no longer necessary (Banet-Weiser, Gill, and Rottenberg 2020). Importantly, however, postfeminism includes the double entanglement of both feminist and antifeminist sentiments. According to McRobbie (2008), elements of feminism have been taken into account and, drawing on a vocabulary that includes words like "empowerment" and "choice," converted into a much more individualistic discourse and deployed as a substitute for feminism, in exchange for intelligibility as women, and the promise of freedom and independence (McRobbie 2008). As McRobbie (2008: 2) argues, "The young woman is offered a notional form of equality, concretised in education and employment, and through participation in consumer culture and civil society, in place of what a reinvented feminist politics might have to offer."

According to Gill (2007), postfeminism includes the notion that femininity is a bodily property; a shift from objectification to subjectification in the ways that certain women (read: Western) are represented; an emphasis on self-surveillance, monitoring, and discipline; a focus on individualism, choice, and empowerment; the dominance of a "makeover paradigm"; a resurgence of ideas of natural sexual difference; the "resexualization" of women's bodies; and an emphasis on consumerism and the commodification of difference. These elements are evident in the rise of the self-help industry, particularly regarding the dating and relationship advice literature intended to help women navigate "innate gender differences" of communication and sensibility (Ward 2020); the rise and proliferation of discourses of sexual entrepreneurship and agency (Attwood 2011; Harvey and Gill 2011); and the increasing popularity and respectability of cosmetic surgery and beauty culture, and their framing as sources of empowerment and emancipation (Lazar 2011; Tincknell 2011).

The emphasis on individualism, choice, and empowerment, while, again, heavily influenced by the individualistic discourse of neoliberalism, takes on new significance under postfeminism, in that women's "choices" and behaviors are strategically divorced from their political and cultural underpinnings. Instead, such choices are framed as evidence of women's liberation in their pursuit of happiness, fulfillment, and empowerment. What is key, however, is that any such empowerment is individualized rather than extended to women as a group, and that those who benefit most from such empowerment—white, upper-class, thin, able-bodied, heterosexual women—are those who already benefit from the interlocking systems of privilege provided by white supremacy and heteropatriarchy (Collins 2002; Cottom 2018; Ward 2020). Through the lens of postfeminism, any such inequities are reduced to personal failings and/or a lack of hard work and investment in the self.

Doing Gender

West and Zimmerman's (1987) "doing gender" theory conceives of gender as an ongoing, interactional accomplishment. Through this lens, gender is not a fixed property of the sexed body but rather a social process of managing one's behaviors and identity in accordance with one's sex category (West and Zimmerman 2009). Normative expectations for men and women maintain gender inequality by encouraging men to "do dominance" and women to "do submission" (Schilt and Westbrook 2009). Accordingly, feminist scholars have celebrated instances where individuals work to "undo" (Deutsch 2007; Risman 2009) or "redo" (West and Zimmerman 2009) gender by challenging the essentialism of gender as a fixed property of the sexed body.

Applications of "doing gender" theory (West and Zimmerman 1987) in women's

sports have revealed that women athletes face competing expectations from sport and

society—a phenomenon that has been described as the "female-athlete paradox" (Felshin

1974; Krane et al. 2004). Understanding how women athletes resist gendered

expectations through participation in "masculine" sports is, therefore, of great importance

for understanding "masculine" sports as sites of empowerment. Because MMA is

strongly associated with male bodies and masculinity, it has been theorized that women's

participation in MMA holds particularly subversive value (Channon and Jennings 2013;

Channon 2014). As such, WMMA has been understood as a potentially powerful site

through which women athletes may become empowered through their resistance to

gendered norms and expectations.

Intersectionality

While "doing gender" theory (West and Zimmerman 1987) is highly appropriate

for analyzing WMMA athletes' gender performances, illuminating the mechanisms that

maintain gender inequality requires a more thorough analysis of the interplay between

gender and sexuality (Schilt and Westbrook 2009), as well as between gender and other

factors, such as race and class (Collins 2002; Combahee River Collective 1974;

Crenshaw 1991). I, therefore, analyzed WMMA athletes' gender performances through

an intersectional feminist lens, which theorizes gender as always intersecting with other

social structures rather than existing in a vacuum (Collins 2002; Combahee River

Collective 1977; Crenshaw 1991).

According to Crenshaw (1991: 1468), to the extent to which feminist theory has

addressed race at all, there has been a historical tendency to view race as an additional

burden in women of color's lives, "one that simply adds to gender oppression rather than

being a part of it." Yet Crenshaw (1991) argues that race cannot be separated from gender

in women of color's lives because race in many ways both shapes the kinds of gender

subordination they experience and limits opportunities for them to successfully challenge

it. This echoes an earlier argument by the Combahee River Collective who stressed the

need to develop an "integrated analysis and practice based upon the fact that the major

systems of oppression are interlocking" (1977: 210). Sports scholars adopting this

approach have revealed many earlier feminist sports inquiries to have extrapolated the

experiences of white women athletes to those of all women athletes and have used the

framework of intersectionality to show how the intersections of gender, race, class, and

sexuality create vastly different outcomes for women athletes depending on their social

locations. This study, therefore, adopts an intersectional feminist approach to better

attend to the intersections of gender, race, class, and sexuality that my study participants

experience and construct a more accurate account of the "empowerment" potential of

WMMA.

POSITIONALITY

My interest in researching WMMA athletes was motivated by nearly fifteen years

of experience in the sport of MMA, where I have participated as both an athlete and a

coach. Routinely seeing depictions of WMMA as "transgressive" and "empowering,"

following women's entrée into the UFC, I found myself unable to reconcile these accounts with what I had experienced as an overtly conservative and misogynistic field. I, therefore, set out to understand how women's participation in MMA impacted their personal lives and to what extent we should characterize this new sport as "empowering."

As a cis, white, heterosexual man and former MMA athlete studying a diverse group of women MMA athletes, I occupied the research position of "insider/outsider" (Dwyer and Buckle 2009). In other words, while my many years of experience in the sport of MMA afforded me invaluable insight into the lives of MMA athletes, my understanding of their world was nevertheless shaped by my experiences as a cis, white, heterosexual man, making my experiences in MMA qualitatively different than those of my study participants. This required me to be reflexive and take into account how my social location impacted my analysis, as well as how it influenced my study participants' impressions of me. In presenting my findings, then, I heed the advice of many feminist scholars to "let women speak" as much as possible by presenting them in the words of the women, themselves. I also, however, heed Smith's (1986: 6) contention that,

> a sociology for women must be able to disclose for women how their own social situation, their everyday world is organized and determined by social processes which are not knowable through the ordinary means through which we find our everyday world.

I, therefore, critically engage with these women's voices to situate their narratives within a broader sociological discourse of gender, sexuality, and power.

While I engage critically with these athletes' beliefs about gender, feminism, and social inequality, this analysis is intended to be read as a critique of the ideologies that *shape* these beliefs rather than a critique of any individual women, themselves. Following the work of critical scholars who understand ideology to be a barrier to liberation, this work is intended to be a profeminist and anti-racist project aimed at critiquing the ideologies that shape subjectivities in MMA and, increasingly, American society. In "talking back" to these ideologies, I hope to use my experience as an MMA subject to make visible the ways in which these ideologies serve to maintain social inequality.

THE BENEFITS OF QUALITATIVE RESEARCH

At a time in which society is experiencing multiple social crises—including a once-in-a-century global pandemic—what is the value of qualitative research? At a time in which the problems of society are seemingly being shaped by macro-level events and phenomena, what is the value of speaking with individual persons? At a time in which the United States is experiencing a rise of fascist politics and ideology (Stanley 2020), women are experiencing the greatest erosion of their reproductive rights in 50 years (Enten 2022), and nearly 41 million Americans believe that the United States is being controlled by a cabal of Satan-worshipping pedophiles (Public Religion Research Institute 2022), what is the value of studying *WMMA athletes*?

These are some of the questions I found myself asking while conducting research on WMMA following the events of 2020. But what became clear to me throughout the course of this project is the immense value of qualitative research for understanding human subjectivity and, consequently, the ideologies that shape human subjectivities and influence social behaviors. Throughout my research, I watched and listened as my research subjects revealed to me the many contradictions in their way of thinking about the world. But as patterns started to emerge from my data, what became clearer to me were the contradictions inherent in the ideologies that shaped these athletes' worldviews.

By studying human subjects through qualitative research methods such as interviewing and ethnography, the researcher is offered a reflection of the various discourses and ideologies that permeate a given culture at a particular point in time and, as such, is offered an intimate view of the relationship between "history and biography" (Mills 1959) in society. Accordingly, qualitative research methodology holds immense value for understanding individuals' resistance to progressive social change. By illuminating the contradictions of the status quo, the qualitative researcher is able to offer a discursive counter to the ideological forces that maintain social inequality and, in turn, contribute to the reader's development of a more critical consciousness. As such, qualitative research holds great value for helping the public achieve social consciousness and allowing the researcher to use their work toward the betterment of society.

THE ROLE OF HISTORY IN SHAPING ETHNOGRAPHIES

My experience conducting this research also revealed to me the unique role of history in shaping ethnographic studies. Both my research subjects' and my experiences were greatly impacted by the Trump presidency and the increasingly hostile "culture wars" in American society, the COVID-19 pandemic and the rise of conspiracy theories in the United States, and the January 6th Capitol Insurrection. This project is, therefore, forever shaped by these events.

While greater attention to positionality and reflexivity in sociology has led to important developments in ethnographic research (Burawoy 2003; Rios 2017), attention to historical context in many contemporary ethnographies is relatively lacking. There is, for instance, often little discussion of the historical forces shaping the socio-political landscape in which these studies occurred, or how these forces impacted the experiences of the research subjects as well as the researcher conducting the study. As I began my interviews with WMMA athletes in 2017, many of these initial interviews featured references to the historic women's march of 2016, or the cultural issues of the day (such as the pervasive anti-trans discourse that became more prominent around this time). Later, as I collected social media data in 2020 and 2021, I observed many more references to the COVID-19 pandemic, the politics of "free speech" and "cancel culture," and vaccines. To attribute these findings to the uniqueness of MMA culture, then, would be a mistake. Rather, as I argue, such findings demonstrate the influence of history on human subjectivity and, correspondingly, the findings of ethnographic studies.

It should be stated then that this project represents one particular ethnographic account of a developing sport at a particularly complicated time in American (and world) history. It makes no claims to be an "objective" scientific view but rather acknowledges Haraway's (1988: 589) argument that science always represents a particular "view from a body, always a complex, contradictory, structuring, and structured body."

FEMINIST THEORY AND PRAXIS

An important feminist tenet is the notion that feminism includes both theory and praxis. As articulated by McCaughey (1997: 200), "that's what makes feminism a theory as well as a social movement." But despite this acknowledgement, much of feminist theory has remained hidden behind journal paywalls or left to collect dust on the shelves of university libraries. The effects of this are that the public often has little (if any) knowledge of feminist theory, and what little understanding they do have of feminism has been warped beyond recognition by patriarchal mass media (hooks 2000). If feminist and profeminist scholars are ever going to work toward real change, then, as Johnson (2004: 25) tells us, "it's a confusion we'll have to clear up."

Profeminist scholars must do a better job of using their work to counter the lies people are being told about feminism. And in order for profeminist scholars to better use their work to influence real-world change, we must do a better job of connecting with the public. We must meet the public where they are. We need to be writing not just about Donald Trump, Bret Kavanaugh, and Harvey Weinstein, but also about Joe Rogan, Alex Jones, Andrew Tate, and anyone else who uses their influence to spread lies about feminism and other social justice movements while hawking CBD oil and cryptocurrencies to their (white, male) audiences. We need to be attacking these people not just for their blatant misogyny but also for their sheer ignorance and utter dishonesty. We need to call out their lies before they become truths. Above all, we need to pay attention.

CHAPTER III: RISE AND GRIND: WMMA CULTURE, POLITICS, AND SUBJECTHOOD

I am sitting in the middle deck of a 17,000-seat arena in Los Angeles, California, waiting for a fight to begin. Beastie Boys' "Girls" is blaring through the arena and there is a woman standing in the middle of a cage wearing a sports bra that says, "Girls fight harder." Another woman is now walking toward the cage to the familiar sounds of rapper, Cardi B. In a few moments, the fight will begin.

At the start of the bell, the fighter to my left sprints across the cage and takes her opponent to the ground. Within moments, she's secured a mounted triangle. She's having difficulty finishing the strangle so she decides to rain down a series of punches and elbows in hopes of knocking her opponent out or forcing the referee to stop the fight. She doesn't get the finish, but she establishes her dominance in what should surely be scored a 10-8 round. As the bell sounds, the referee separates the two athletes and motions them back to their respective corners. While the first round comes to a close, No Doubt's "I'm Just a Girl" booms throughout the arena.

INTRODUCTION

There is much to be gained from a thorough sociological examination of women's mixed martial arts (WMMA). Situated at the intersection of combat sports and entertainment, WMMA offers unique insights into the evolving dynamics of gender, sexuality, and violence in modern sport and society. Scholars have argued that WMMA holds potential for the empowerment of women, as well as for the wider subversion of patriarchal gender norms throughout society (Jakubowska, Channon and Matthews 2016;

Jennings 2015, Mierzwinski, Velija, and Malcolm 2014, Weaving 2015). Indeed, such has been the primary framing of women's mixed martial arts.

While the scholarship on WMMA has been informative, little has been written about the socio-cultural and political world of WMMA, as well as the unique subjecthood of WMMA athletes. While studies such as Spencer (2009), Abramson and Modzelewski (2011), and Green (2016) have no doubt informed us about much of MMA culture, these studies all took place before women had begun participating in major MMA promotions and, therefore, focused primarily on the experiences of male athletes and MMA's relationship to masculinity. While these scholars' insights are important, there remains much to learn about the present-day culture of WMMA, as well as the new women athletes who occupy this violent sport.

In this chapter, I discuss the culture, politics, and subjecthood of WMMA. Drawing from my years of ethnographic study at an MMA academy in Southern California, a content analysis of MMA media, and data from 40 semistructured interviews with WMMA athletes, I offer the most thorough sociological description of WMMA to date and discuss the culture and politics of this developing sport. I also discuss the unique subjecthood of WMMA athletes and share their perspectives on whether or not they experience WMMA as a site of empowerment and "physical feminism" (McCaughey 1997). Finally, I propose an original concept, which I refer to as "the breaking barriers paradox," to conceptualize the ways in which women's participation in MMA has been framed as both a source of women's empowerment and a celebration of women's liberation.

SETTING THE SCENE

What is Mixed Martial Arts (MMA)?

Mixed martial arts (MMA) is a full-contact combat sport where athletes compete against one another in hand-to-hand combat wearing minimal clothing; small, 4-ounce, fingerless gloves; a mouthpiece; and a protective cup (for male athletes). Athletes seek to attain victory by knocking their opponents out, forcing their opponents to "submit," scoring "technical knockout outs (TKOs)" by rendering their opponents unable to "intelligently" defend themselves, or by winning "judges' decisions" based on the scoring criteria of effective striking, effective grappling, aggression, and cage control. Most MMA promotions utilize boxing's "10-9" scoring system (where the winner of each round is awarded ten "points" while their opponent is awarded nine "points" or fewer), although some promotions—such as the Singapore-based ONE Championship—employ different scoring systems and criteria. MMA is most commonly associated with the premier MMA organization—Ultimate Fighting Championship (UFC)—and is colloquially referred to as "cage fighting" or "ultimate fighting" by outside observers.

While MMA was originally developed as a contest between martial artists of competing martial arts disciplines in an attempt to prove which style would be most effective in a "real-world" hand-to-hand fight, MMA has since evolved into an amalgamation of these once competing disciplines, requiring modern MMA athletes to be competent (if not proficient) in a variety of martial arts, including Brazilian Jiu-Jitsu, wrestling, boxing, and muay Thai, as well as others. The modern MMA academy will typically offer classes in Brazilian Jiu-Jitsu (where athletes develop skills in the area of grappling and submission fighting), wrestling (where athletes learn to ground their opponents through leg tackles and upper body throws), boxing (where athletes work diligently on their footwork and punching skills to develop timing, speed, and accuracy), and muay Thai (where athletes learn to attack with the so-called "eight limbs" of hands, feet, knees, and elbows). Most MMA academies will also typically feature "sparring days" where no group classes are held but rather athletes compete against one another in a semi-controlled fashion to work on combining the various skills they acquire and testing them against resistance before using them in competition. MMA academies also typically hold "drilling sessions," where athletes practice a particular range of skills, such as wrestling up against the cage wall or working to get back to a standing position after being pinned to the ground.

The sport of MMA features both amateur and professional competition. While elite MMA organizations like the UFC or ONE Championship will typically only include professional bouts, most regional and national MMA events are comprised of both amateur and professional fights. Athletes will typically compete several times as amateurs before "turning pro," although some athletes enter directly into professional competition—usually because of their professional experience in another combat sport, such as boxing or Brazilian Jiu-Jitsu. In some jurisdictions, however, athletes are actually required to compete several times as amateurs before being granted a license to compete as a professional.

Recently, MMA has surpassed boxing to become the most popular combat sport in the world (Cheever 2009). Vaulted into the mainstream by the success of the UFC,

MMA is now a highly visible and widely accepted form of sports entertainment. Indeed, sports *entertainment* is the most appropriate way to conceptualize the sport of MMA, as MMA contests are not beholden to a "tournament" or "league" structure and are organized around fan interest rather than merit. In this sense, the business structure of MMA is more closely aligned with sports such as boxing or professional wrestling than it is with other major sports like football, basketball, and baseball. Like boxing and professional wrestling, major MMA events are also typically sold as pay-per-view "cards," while smaller events are broadcast on sports television channels and online.

An important distinction between MMA and boxing, however, is that while viewership in boxing is largely determined by the popularity of individual athletes, MMA viewership is much more determined by the popularity of the promotions hosting the events. This severely limits the bargaining power of MMA athletes and is an important factor in the UFC's monopolistic control over the MMA industry. Because the UFC's success is largely divorced from the popularity of their athletes, there is little incentive for the UFC to sign athletes to contracts that do not overwhelmingly favor the promotion. In fact, former-co-owner of the UFC, Lorenzo Fertitta, famously stated about his purchase of the UFC in 2001, that he essentially bought three letters: U, F, C. This statement highlights the fact that Fertitta understood the unique appeal of the UFC's brand, which has led to the UFC's being viewed synonymously with the sport of MMA. In fact, in the UFC's 20-year anniversary documentary, *Fighting for a Generation: 20 Years of the UFC* (2013), Fertitta defends his statement, explaining that, "People were not walking down the street saying, 'Hey, I wanna' buy this mixed martial arts pay-per-view.' People said, 'I wanna' buy the *UFC* pay-per-view.'" This remains an important

distinction between MMA and boxing today, as well as between the UFC and other

MMA promotions.

What is Women's Mixed Martial Arts (WMMA)?

While modern MMA events typically feature both male and female bouts,

women's mixed martial arts, or WMMA, is the term commonly used to describe

women's participation in MMA. Unlike women's boxing, however, women MMA

athletes compete under the same rules and conditions as men, and often earn similar pay.

Although women previously competed in shorter rounds (Mierzwinski, Velija, and

Malcolm 2014), since 2009, women and men have competed under the same ruleset,

contributing to MMA's reputation as an "even playing field" for women athletes (see, for

example, Head 2016; Martin 2019).

While women do not compete against men in MMA competition, it is not usual

for women to train (and even spar) with men of varying size, strength, and skill in their

respective MMA academies. Indeed, several scholars have highlighted this fact to

illustrate the subversive potential of women's participation in MMA, as it allows (or at

least appears to allow) athletes to dispel myths about women's vulnerability, lack of

physical strength, and supposed inability to engage in physical aggression (Channon

2014; Channon and Jennings 2013; Mierzwinski, Velija, and Malcolm 2014). Similarly,

scholars have posited that the intimate nature of mixed-gender training provides

opportunities to queer boundaries between genders and sexualities (Channon 2014;

Channon and Jennings 2013), particularly in grappling sessions where athletes of different genders are often positioned in sexually-suggestive ways. Indeed, the following

vignette from my field notes illustrates the subversive potential of the MMA academy, as

well as the juxtaposition of norms WMMA so often provides.

> *I am sitting on the mat at the South Side Training Academy while waiting for Friday sparring to begin. The big garage doors that separate the training area from the parking lot are open today and the cool breeze cutting through the thick, hot air of the gym feels nice on this hot, summer day. There is a pit bull tied to the chain link fence that borders the mats, barking at passersby as they peer through the fence to get a glimpse of the fighters as they shadowbox in anticipation of the violence that is set to begin. Suddenly, a fighter yells out from across the room, "Wait! I need to go change my tampon!" "Welcome to women's MMA," another fighter leans over to say to me, her amusement matching my own.*

At first glance, WMMA appears to offer the same subversive potential that has

been discussed in sports such as roller derby (Finley 2010; Gieseler 2014) and women's

rugby (Broad 2001; Chase 2006). Indeed, there is a curious blend of masculinity,

femininity, sexuality, and violence that sets WMMA apart from many women's sports. It

is my argument, however, that much of this juxtaposition is for show. As it will become

clear throughout this dissertation, *the paradox is the point* (I will elaborate this particular

point further in Chapter 4, as I explicate my original concept, "doing both").

It is important to remember that MMA is a multi-billion-dollar industry. In fact,

like boxing, MMA is often referred to by its participants as "the fight business." And

while individual women may discover MMA through motivations for personal fitness or

self-defense, the athletes who compete in MMA are "prize fighters" and participate in

MMA primarily for profit. In fact, a popular expression used by men and women athletes

in MMA is "if it makes dollars, it makes sense"—an expression often used to justify

MMA athletes' decisions to accept certain MMA bouts while turning down others.

Professional MMA athletes' behaviors, then—regardless of gender—should be interpreted, at least, in part, through this lens.

South Side Training Academy (SSTA)

My primary research site for this dissertation was the South Side Training Academy (SSTA) in Southern California. The members of SSTA included martial arts hobbyists training for self-defense and personal fitness; amateur MMA, Brazilian Jiu-Jitsu, muay Thai, wrestling, and boxing competitors looking to sharpen their skills before joining the ranks of the professionals; and professional MMA athletes, including some of the sport's most accomplished fighters. I chose SSTA specifically because of the fact that it is home to one of the largest *women* MMA competition teams in the United States. In fact, women athletes from across the United States routinely travel to SSTA for "sparring sessions," as sparring sessions at SSTA typically include many more women with whom to spar than is the case at most MMA academies.

While SSTA is known primarily for its women athletes, the vast majority of the coaches employed by SSTA are men. Like most MMA academies, the women who do serve in coaching roles at SSTA are usually relegated to coaching children or "women-only" classes. The men who coach at SSTA are comprised primarily of active and retired competitors from the sports of MMA, boxing, wrestling, and Brazilian Jiu-Jitsu. Because coaches are seen as authority figures in MMA, it is not uncommon for them to adopt paternal roles in their students' lives—particularly when their students are women. The head coach of the WMMA competition team at SSTA, in fact, jokingly refers to himself as "The Broadfather" and has a reputation for being a successful mentor to women MMA fighters, in particular.

A monthly membership at SSTA costs approximately one hundred and fifty dollars per month. Women, however, are sometimes permitted to train for free, as they are harder to recruit than men and are seen as valuable training partners for SSTA's women competitors who often have fewer female bodies with which to train. SSTA will sometimes even advertise free training for women in their promotional materials to further their efforts to recruit women athletes. These efforts have proven successful for their academy and have earned them a reputation for having some of the toughest women around.

The Mean Girls

The group of women who represent SSTA in professional and amateur MMA competition colloquially refer to themselves as "The Mean Girls." A reference to the film, *Mean Girls* (2004), the moniker distinguishes these women from the rest of the athletes at SSTA, as both *fighters* and *women*. The Mean Girls group, therefore, does not include women who merely participate at SSTA as students or practitioners, nor does it include the men from SSTA who compete as fighters in MMA competition. The Mean Girls group is reserved rather for women fighters from SSTA who choose to identify themselves as such and have been welcomed into the group by its other members.

"Teams" in MMA, however, are largely symbolic and it is not uncommon for "teammates" to fight one another in MMA competition. A distinguishing aspect of MMA culture is, in fact, that teammates routinely compete against one another. While, to my knowledge, none of the fighters in The Mean Girls group have ever competed against one another, I have observed several of the athletes on more than one occasion discuss the potential of fighting their teammates and express a willingness to do so. I have also witnessed several of the athletes experience visible tension with one another, with "sparring" sessions sometimes erupting into real fights, and with some athletes earning reputations as "bad teammates."

Throughout my time at SSTA, I also witnessed several of the athletes get kicked out of the academy (and subsequentially off of the team) for being disrespectful to their coaches or for other personal reasons. On one occasion, it was explained to me that a member of The Mean Girls had been kicked off the team due to her sleeping with a member of a rival Brazilian Jiu-Jitsu team. As explained to me by a member of The Mean Girls, "[Coach] was like, 'It's not bad enough that they're beating us in jiu-jitsu, now they're fucking our women?'" Nevertheless, the "team" element of MMA—be it in the "official" capacity as members of a particular MMA academy or in less official ways such as The Mean Girls sub-team—is an important aspect of the MMA experience and further distinguishes it from the training culture of boxing.

WMMA CULTURE

Neoliberalism

MMA culture is, perhaps above all, a powerful site for the reproduction of neoliberal capitalist values. Discourses of hard work, personal sacrifice, and meritocracy all circulate throughout MMA culture, and slogans, such as "rise and grind," "embrace the grind," and "earned, not given," provide fertile ideological fodder for neoliberal tenets of personal responsibility, personal sacrifice, and the rejection of public welfare. MMA culture encourages neoliberal self-help practices like "mindfulness," "visualization," and "manifesting," as habits for success, and encourages the MMA subject to "pull themselves up by their bootstraps" rather than "being a victim." In this way, MMA discourse instills in its subjects an ideology of individualism that blinds them to social inequality and occupies their minds with projects of the self. It should come as no surprise, then, that MMA is commonly referred to by its participants as a "selfish sport" (I will elaborate this particular point further in a later section of this chapter).

A common sentiment shared among MMA athletes is the idea that "the only one who can prevent you from achieving your goals is *you*." MMA athletes, then, tend to focus their energy and attention inward rather than considering how outside factors may contribute to their circumstances. When an athlete wins a fight, for example, they will often cite their "hard work," "personal sacrifice," or "determination" as reasons for their victory, while also overlooking other factors that may have contributed to their success. By the same token, when an athlete loses a fight, they are encouraged to take "ownership" for their loss rather than point the blame elsewhere. Even in instances where outside factors clearly intervene (say, for example, in the case of an erroneous judges' decision), MMA culture assigns blame to the athletes, themselves, rather than to the officials or the promoter (as demonstrated by the popular expression, "Never leave it in the hands of the judges").

An examination of WMMA athletes' social media reveals the ideological workings of neoliberalism on WMMA athletes' sensibilities and behaviors. Take, for instance, the following statements shared by WMMA athletes on social media.

> "If you condition yourself to see everything in life as training, your suffering will disappear."

> "It's on *you*, to get *you*, where *you*, need to be."

> "We need to fill our cups first before we fill others'."

> "Visualize. Until it becomes reality."

> "The outcome of your life is in your hands. Don't blame anyone or anything else. You are the captain of your ship, MASTER YOUR DESTINY!!"

Consistent among these statements is the emphasis on the self as the source of one's failures and successes. Rather than calling attention to the injustice of one's circumstances, then, the MMA subject is encouraged to look inward and alter their "mindset" while accepting any such injustices as "training" or "lessons" on their path toward empowerment. The popular MMA expression, "pain is temporary, glory is forever," perhaps, best encapsulates this point, and further demonstrates the overlaps between neoliberal ideology and MMA culture; while putting one's body through arduous exercise and pain in training may be temporary unpleasant (or even torturous), the "glory" of victory or of "being the best" will render one's sacrifices worthwhile in the end.

MMA athletes' neoliberal sensibilities are also reinforced by their coaches who, like them, have had their subjectivities shaped by neoliberal culture. Consider the following social media statements shared by some of the most influential coaches in

MMA.

> "If you are looking for that one person who can change your life…Have a look in
> the mirror."

> "Stop blaming other people…Realize and accept that life isn't fair."

> "*'I identify as a Hard Worker, have watched others work hard, read about it, and
> believe I should be given what they've earned.'* I believe you are a total dipshit
> and are about to get paid in knuckles, and earn some well-deserved abrasions,
> bruises and scars."

Consistent among these statements is the emphasis on hard work and personal

responsibility as the source of one's success. Through this logic, what separates

"winners" and "losers," then, is the amount of work one is "willing" to put in to achieve

victory rather than other factors like ability, resources, or time. This contributes to a

culture of victim-blaming and the tendency for MMA athletes to view (and speak of)

themselves as exceptional individuals who are simply willing to work harder than those

around them.

Influencers

The influence of neoliberal ideology on MMA culture is evident in the increasing

overlaps between MMA and other neoliberal industries, such as the wellness industry, the

self-help industry, the stand-up comedy industry, and the podcasting industry. Cultural

"influencers" like Joe Rogan, Jordan Peterson, and "Jocko" Willink are among the most

celebrated figures in MMA, and all of these figures routinely promote neoliberal tenets of

hard work and personal responsibility, as well as popular neoliberal self-help concepts like "human potential" and "human optimization." In the following section, I examine these "influencers" and their relationships to MMA culture.

Joe Rogan

It would be difficult to overstate the influence Joe Rogan has on the MMA community. Indeed, it would not be an exaggeration to say that he is the most beloved figure in the sport. I have heard his name innumerable times throughout this project. I have heard it at SSTA, at my own academy, on social media, on television, at local fights, at major fights, in a taxi on the way to the arena, in the fighter van on the way to the airport, in the airport, in the United States, in Malaysia, in Singapore, and even backstage preparing my athlete to fight. Rogan's brand and ideas are ubiquitous throughout MMA culture.

The MMA community's affinity for Joe Rogan can be described as a cult of personality. In fact, Rogan's Instagram account features many photos of fans (almost entirely men) who have even gotten his face tattooed on their bodies, often accompanied by related elements of Rogan's brand, such as apes, magic mushrooms, and marijuana leaves. His podcast, "The Joe Rogan Experience," is the number one podcast in the world and it has served to bolster the careers of many an MMA athlete. The "rub"—or informal granting of credibility—that one gets from associating with Rogan (and especially from being featured as a guest on his podcast) has, in fact, gotten so extreme that it has actually developed into a small problem for the UFC in recent years, as UFC athletes are increasingly using their post-fight in-cage interviews with Rogan to request to be guests on his podcast rather than actually answering his questions. These in-cage interviews have led to some bizarre moments in recent years, including WMMA athlete, Vanessa Demopoulos, jumping into his arms after her victory over Silvana Gomez Juarez, and WMMA athlete, Jessica Eye, asking him, "You can look at my butt, but why don't you have me on your podcast?" after her victory over Katlyn Chookagian.

Although Rogan himself has never competed in MMA, his black belt in Brazilian Jiu-Jitsu, prior experience as an amateur kickboxer, and longstanding role as UFC color commentator have allowed him to achieve "insider" status in the MMA community and have earned him a reputation as a "manly man" throughout wider popular culture. Indeed, Rogan's association with MMA and "men's issues" like "cancel culture," "wokeness," and the broader "feminization" of society have allowed him to, perhaps more so than anyone else alive at the time of this writing, represent (white, hetero)masculinity in the contemporary United States. Among the most discussed topics on his podcast are fighting, hunting, and "social justice warriors."

Social justice warrior, or "SJW," is a pejorative term used to describe someone who expresses or promotes progressive social views (Phelan 2019). Originally popularized by alt-right and far-right actors on internet platforms like 4chan, 8Chan, and Reddit, the SJW has since come to represent a cultural figure that is not only ridiculed by the far right, but the target of liberal (and especially neoliberal) critique in general (Phelan 2019). SJWs are said to represent (by those who use the term) an individual who engages in arguments on behalf of social justice, not for altruistic reasons but rather for the purpose of raising their own personal reputation. SJWs', then, are often accused of "virtue signaling," or feigning care for progressive causes for the purpose of "signaling" their moral superiority.

Rogan's critiques of SJWs, as well as other progressive figures like feminists, anti-racists, and "antifa," directly shape how these figures are conceptualized and regarded by members of the MMA community. With some of Rogan's more popular YouTube videos featuring titles like "Joe Rogan vs. Feminist," "Joe Rogan: Feminism is Sexist Towards Women," and "Joe Rogan: Male Feminists Are Weasels" (all videos that, at the time of this writing, have been viewed over 2 million times), it is not difficult to understand how Rogan's work contributes to a culture of anti-feminism in MMA. With other popular YouTube videos featuring Rogan including the titles, "Joe Rogan: When Did SJW Culture Start?" "Joe Rogan: The MAJOR Problem With 'Trans' Women in Sport, Cancel Culture & Social Justice Warriors!!" and "Joe Rogan on Leftist Social Retards & Piranhas," it is also not difficult to understand how Rogan's views contribute to a culture of antisociality in general.

Perhaps, the most famous YouTube video to feature Joe Rogan is hosted by his former wellness supplement company and "lifestyle brand," Onnit. The video, entitled, "Be The Hero of Your Own Movie | Joe Rogan Motivation," features Rogan speaking directly into the camera and offering words of motivation while dramatic music plays in the background. In the video, Rogan states,

> Be the hero of your own movie. If your life was a movie and it started now—
> forget about whatever financial disasters you've had, personal failures,
> relationship failures—what would the hero of your life's movie do right now? Do
> that! Do those things! We define ourselves far too often by our past failures. We
> look at our past and we say, 'Well, that's me.' That's *not* you. You are *this* person
> right now. You're the person who's learned from those failures and you can

choose to be the hero of your movie right now. Write down your goals. Write down things you want to improve. Write down things you won't tolerate from yourself. Write down things from the past that you never want to see yourself do again and go forth from here as the hero of your own movie. Build momentum. Build confidence and momentum with each good decision that you make from here on out. You can do it. *Anyone* can do it. We live in unique times. We live in one of the rarest times in human history where you can choose almost all of the input that comes your way. Whether it's the movies that you watch, the books you read, the podcasts you listen to, you can *choose* to be inspired. Do *that*. Do that and be the hero of your own movie.

Although Rogan's words of encouragement may be helpful to some, the framing of Rogan's intervention places the blame of one's life outcomes squarely on the shoulders of the individual. And while one's individual behavior is undeniably impactful in the outcome of one's life, individual decisions and behaviors, alone, do not determine one's fate. Moreover, the notion that one can simply "forget" about consequential barriers like "financial disasters" effectively amounts to neoliberal gaslighting, or the perpetuation of the idea that social and economic barriers are largely immaterial. In this way, Rogan's brand and ideas serve the perpetuation of the individual-centric thinking common among MMA athletes and contributes to the spread of neoliberal ideology throughout MMA culture.

Jordan Peterson

Ask any MMA fighter who their favorite psychologist is and they will give you one name: Jordan Peterson. Like Rogan, Peterson's brand promotes neoliberal ideals of hard work and personal responsibility, as well as other neoliberal tenets like deregulation and the rejection of public welfare. Peterson—himself a frequent guest on Rogan's podcast—is, perhaps, best known for his book, *12 Rules for Life: An Antidote to Chaos.* Released in 2018, Peterson's *12 Rules for Life* has since grown into a remarkably popular self-help book among men, who are the primary targets of his message. The so-called

"twelve rules" that Peterson advocates to his readers are as follows:

1. Stand up straight with your shoulders back.

2. Treat yourself like you are someone you are responsible for helping.

3. Make friends with people who want the best for you.

4. Compare yourself to who you were yesterday, not to who someone else is today.

5. Do not let your children do anything that makes you dislike them.

6. Set your house in perfect order before you criticize the world.

7. Pursue what is meaningful (not what is expedient).

8. Tell the truth—or, at least, don't lie.

9. Assume that the person you are listening to might know something you don't.

10. Be precise in your speech.

11. Do not bother children while they are skateboarding.

12. Pet a cat when you encounter one in the street.

Like Rogan, Peterson also has a podcast: "The Jordan B. Peterson Podcast."

Among the most discussed topics on his podcast (and, subsequently, in his appearances

on other podcasts) is the topic of gender differences. Often framed as an ideological

counter to "postmodernists" or "the woke mob," Peterson argues that biology rather than

culture is the main determinate of gender differences and that Western society has

underemphasized these differences because of the influences of postmodernism and

feminism. Fearing the future loss of all men and masculinity, Peterson advocates for a

return to "traditional" gender ideals.

Because of his stances against "woke" practices like acknowledging non-binary gender identities and honoring one's preferred gender pronouns, Peterson has earned a reputation as a "controversial thinker" on the "intellectual dark web," garnering him the support of millions of (white) men who view him as one of the great intellectuals of our time. In fact, *The New York Times'* columnist, David Brooks, writing about Peterson in 2018, described him as "the most influential public intellectual in the Western world." Within the MMA community, specifically, the respect for Peterson's intelligence is so great that his name is sometimes used synonymously with the very concept of genius—similar to Albert Einstein's. For example, I have heard, on more than one occasion, an MMA athlete begin a sentence with, "I'm no Jordan Peterson but…," and then make a statement about their intelligence.

Among the more popular videos featuring Jordan Peterson on YouTube include the titles, "Jordan Peterson Completely Destroys Feminist Narrative," "Jordan Peterson Calmly Dismantles Feminism in Front of Two Feminists," and "Jordan Peterson discusses whether men and women can ever be equal." Arguably Peterson's most famous moment, however, comes from his appearance on Channel 4 News on January 16th, 2018, wherein he engaged in a spirited debate with British journalist, Cathy Newman. The video—which, at the time of this writing, has been viewed more than 41 million times—earned Newman heavy criticism due to her repeated use of the phrase, "So, you're saying," and served to bolster Peterson's reputation as a "coolly rational man of science facing down the hysteria of political correctness" (Lynskey 2018). In a particularly contentious exchange, Peterson and Newman discuss what Peterson sees as the gender

pay gap "myth." The exchange goes as follows:

> Newman: If you're a woman and, on average, you're getting paid nine percent less than a man, that's not fair, is it?
>
> Peterson: It depends on why it's happening. I can give you an example. There's a personality trait known as agreeableness. Agreeable people are compassionate and polite. Agreeable people get paid less than less agreeable people for the same job. Women are more agreeable than men.
>
> Newman: Again, a vast generalization.
>
> Peterson: It's not a generalization.
>
> Newman: Some women are not more agreeable than men.
>
> Peterson: Yes, that's true. That's right. And some women get paid more than men.
>
> Newman: So, you're saying that, by and large, women are too agreeable to get the pay raises they deserve?
>
> Peterson. No, I'm saying that's one component of a multivariate equation that predicts salary. It accounts for maybe five percent of the variance—something like that. You need about another eighteen factors—one of which is gender. And there is prejudice. There's no doubt about that. But it accounts for a much smaller proportion of the variance in the pay gap than the radical feminists claim.

Peterson's popularity in the MMA community contributes not only to a culture of

anti-feminism in MMA but also to the common sentiment shared among MMA athletes

that the United States is a meritocracy and that social factors play a much smaller role in

one's success than individual factors like "work ethic" and "determination." This, in

turns, provides ideological support for the neoliberal architecture of the MMA industry

(and that of the UFC, in particular) and contributes to the "cruel optimism" experienced

by MMA athletes (Berlant 2020; McClearen 2021). As such, Peterson's work contributes both to the neoliberal values embedded in MMA culture and to the neoliberal sensibilities of MMA athletes.

"Jocko" Willink

Another highly influential figure in MMA culture is former United States Navy SEAL, John "Jocko" Willink. Willink—a veteran of the Iraq War—originally gained notoriety following the release of his book, *Extreme Ownership: How U.S. Navy Seals Lead and Win,* in 2015. He is the author of several other self-help books, including *Discipline Equals Freedom: Field Manual* (2017) and *The Code. The Evaluation. The Protocols: Striving to Become an Eminently Qualified Human* (2020). He is also the owner of several successful businesses, including the popular wellness supplement line, Jocko Fuel.

Like Peterson, Willink is a frequent guest on "The Joe Rogan Experience." He also has his own podcast: "Jocko Podcast." According to his website, "Jocko Podcast" is dedicated to discussing "discipline and leadership in business, war, relationships, and everyday life" (JockoPodcast.com). At the time of this writing, it has nearly 1.6 million subscribers on YouTube, and his most popular titles include, "Be Dangerous But Disciplined – Jocko Willink & Jordan Peterson," "Why Discipline Must Come From Within – Jocko Willink," and "How To SMASH DAYS When You Don't Feel Like It."

Among the most popular YouTube videos featuring Willink comes from the conservative American advocacy group, PragerU. The video, entitled, "Discipline = Freedom," served as PragerU's 2019 "commencement address" and, at the time of this writing, has been viewed nearly 6 million times. In the video, Willink outlines three "key principles" to follow in order to achieve success in "any arena." They are 1. Discipline equals freedom, 2. Stay humble, and 3. Extreme ownership. In the video, explains his concept of "extreme ownership," stating,

> The third and final principle: take ownership of *everything*. I call this, "extreme ownership." In the military, the best leaders and the best troops were the ones that took ownership of everything in their world, not just the things that they were responsible for but for every challenge and obstacle that impacted their mission. When something went wrong, they cast no blame. They made no excuses. They took ownership of the problem and fixed it. You can implement this attitude as well, not only in your job but *in your life*. Let other people blame their parents, their boss, or "the system." Let weaker people complain that the world isn't fair. You are the leader of your life. Take ownership of everything in it.

Materials like these contribute to the sense shared among MMA fighters that the individual is the sole architect of one's life and that individual factors like "discipline" and "will" are the strongest determinants of one's life outcomes. What this way of thinking overlooks, however, is that social factors like gender, race, and class strongly constrain individuals' abilities to exercise their "will" and achieve success, even despite a "disciplined" work ethic. This is readily apparent in the gender, race, and class makeup of influencers like Rogan, Peterson, and Willink, who have all undoubtedly benefited from their statuses as rich, white men. Nevertheless, these influencers all exert powerful cultural influence over the MMA community and contribute to the endurance of neoliberal hegemony within MMA culture.

Wellness

There are many overlaps between MMA and wellness cultures. Like MMA, wellness is a highly individualized physical cultural space, and, like MMA fighters, wellness practitioners strive to "optimize" their health and reach their "human potential" in the pursuit of being "well." Popular practices like "self-care," "mindfulness," and "positive thinking" are common in each of these industries (Baker 2022), as self-discovery and -transformation are the ultimate goals of each of these physical journeys. Perhaps, nowhere, however, are these overlaps more apparent than in the success of the MMA-wellness-inspired company, Onnit.

Onnit—co-founded by Joe Rogan and business partner, Aubrey Marcus—is a popular "lifestyle brand" among MMA practitioners that sells original supplements like "Alpha BRAIN" and "Shroom Tech," as well as fitness products, apparel, and "Onnit Certified Trainer" courses (Onnit.com). An examination of Onnit's website reveals many of the influences of MMA and wellness cultures, including not only many references to "alternative" health and fitness practices (Baker 2022) but also numerous images of MMA athletes. Like MMA—and women's MMA, in particular—Onnit also frames its mission as one of "empowerment," and centers the "individual" as its primary unit of analysis. For example, on Onnit's website, it states,

> We are on a mission to empower as many individuals as possible with a holistic philosophy regarding physical, mental, and spiritual well-being. We believe that if people have access to the best tools and knowledge, they will be able to achieve their fullest human potential, leading to a global movement for the good of all.

While Onnit identifies its goal as "empowerment" for the "good of all," its individual-centered focus reveals the trappings of neoliberalism (Gill and Scharff 2013). Similarly, a video on Onnit's website, entitled, "What is Onnit?" features many neoliberal "self-empowerment" tropes, including the focus on the self as the source of one's failures and successes, references to "bootstrap pulling" or "picking oneself back up," and the symbolism of powerful bodies overcoming obstacles to communicate empowerment. The video, in fact, includes several images of MMA athletes hitting pads,

as well as other athletic bodies "breaking through" by successfully lifting weights or

sprinting to the finish (with the help of Onnit's products). In it, the narrator states,

> You know who you are. And who you wanna' *become*. Uncertainty and failure
> stand before you. But the biggest obstacle is *you*. How do you handle adversity?
> How many times can you fall and still pull yourself back up? What do you do
> when no one else is around? What do you do when you get tired, unmotivated,
> and you don't "feel like it?" When you want to quit, do you take a breath and
> *focus*? Only the journey matters. There are only the moments that take you closer
> to who you want to become. Moments that make you a little bit better today than
> yesterday. And the only way to get there is *you*. Are you up for it?

An original concept integrated into Onnit's brand is what co-founder, Aubrey

Marcus, terms, "Total Human Optimization (THO)." According to Marcus, THO can be

described as,

> a commitment to get strong in the places where we are weak, become great in
> places where we're good, and shine a light on the stuff we need to take a look at.
> Most importantly, THO is about recognizing that nothing works in a vacuum. You
> have to bring it all together if you want to maximize what's possible.

THO, then, can be conceptualized as an approach that includes not only daily practice,

but also a "commitment" to improving oneself over time. This approach has much in

common with MMA training, where the MMA subject is encouraged to strive to get "one

percent better" each day and view their training as a "journey" rather than a

"destination." In fact, on Onnit's website, under the subheading, "What is the purpose of

total human optimization," it reads,

> Optimization is a process and not a prize. A journey—not a destination. To be
> truly optimized is to live up to your potential at any given moment. At the same
> time, we recognize that your potential today is not the same as it will be in a year
> if you stay the course, so to judge yourself today on the standards of tomorrow is
> foolhardy. To start optimizing effectively now, you only have to recognize that
> the mind, body, and spirit are interconnected.

Like the MMA subject, then, the Onnit consumer is encouraged to see their daily practices as a "lifestyle"—both for the ever-present goal of "optimization" and for the ever-precarious goal of being "well."

Masculinity

Like other combat sports, MMA culture is heavily influenced by hegemonic masculine ideals (Connell 2013; Connell and Messerschmidt 2005). Indeed, numerous scholars have highlighted MMA's relationship to masculinity (Abramson and Modzelewski 2011; Bowman 2020; Green 2016; Hirose and Pih 2010; Spencer 2013; Vaccaro, Schrock, and McCabe 2011) and its framing by its participants as a space for "real" men (Bowman 2020; Hirose and Pih 2010; Vaccaro, Schrock, and McCabe 2011). It has been posited that because of masculinity's association with violence (Kimmel 2013; Messner 1990) and MMA's framing as the "truest" test of one's fighting ability, MMA holds particularly high stakes for "proving" one's masculinity (Jakubowska, Channon, and Matthews 2016). MMA culture, therefore, exemplifies many elements of hypermasculinity (Bowman 2020).

Discourses of "power," "fearlessness," and "durability" are all used to communicate masculine ideals throughout MMA culture. Other "masculine" symbols like guns, cars, and money are also used to display male fighters' masculinity both in person and on social media. Fighters will often attempt to emasculate their opponents by questioning their power, "chin" (i.e., ability to take a punch), or sexuality, or even taunting their opponents in the cage with symbolic acts of dominance like "humping" them from behind. Misogynistic and homophobic slurs like "pussy," "faggot," and "bitch" are, therefore, common insults in MMA and are used to call an opponent's masculinity (and sexuality) into question.

The influence of hegemonic masculine ideals can also be observed in the daily training practices of MMA athletes. Ignoring pain and training through injuries, for example, is a common practice among MMA athletes, as "pulling out" of fights (due to injury or otherwise) is considered a shameful (and "unmanly") act. "Missing weight," or weighing in above the contracted weight limit, is also considered shameful, as it is understood to communicate a lack of "discipline," "professionalism," and pain tolerance.

So, too, is fighting in a way that displays restraint or caution, as fighters are expected to "leave it all in the cage," even if it means risking being knocked out or sustaining considerable brain damage. In the UFC, for example, fighters who employ a strategic or cautious approach have often earned the ire of President, Dana White, who encourages fighters to "lay it all on the line" or risk being cut by the promotion. In some cases, White has even left the arena before the completion of a night's "main event" due to a fight's being "boring," or refused to place the UFC's championship belt around champions who have won fights in "unexciting" ways. Expressions like "just bleed"—a reference to a UFC fan who went viral after being featured on the UFC 15 broadcast with the words "UFC" painted on his forehead and the words "Just Bleed" painted on his bare chest—and "Let me bang, bro!"—a reference to former TUF contestant, Julian Lane, drunkenly screaming the now famous phrase through tears as his teammates restrained him from assaulting another cast member—are, therefore, commonly used by MMA athletes to communicate the style of fighting that is most appreciated by MMA fans and promoters.

Women's participation in the UFC and other promotions has done little to challenge the masculine character of MMA. The sex-segregated structure of MMA has limited women MMA athletes' ability to challenge the presumed superiority of male MMA athletes, and the small range of weight classes available to women—115lbs to 145lbs in the UFC—has ensured that women MMA athletes' bodies are relatively small and coded "feminine" by fans and observers. Women's achievements in MMA are, therefore, relatively unthreatening to the masculine status of most male observers who (falsely) presume that they would be able to merely overpower the women who compete in MMA. Retired UFC athlete, David "Tank" Abbott, for example, claimed in 2014 that not only would the then-50-year-old Abbott beat "any woman on Earth," but that even Ronda Rousey would not be a challenge for him due to her being "a girl," and that he would make Rousey "make [him] a sandwich" after beating her (Lyles 2015). Fan comments on social media also serve to limit the symbolic challenge of WMMA athletes' achievements to the dominance of men and masculinity by either accusing the athletes of being men (or challenging their statuses as "real" women) or disparaging them in other ways (such as by criticizing their appearance or questioning their competence).

The persistence of hegemonic masculinity throughout MMA culture is evident in the MMA community's affinity for cultural figures who are associated with hegemonic masculine ideals, such as Joe Rogan, "Jocko" Willink, and Andrew Tate, as well as in MMA athletes' and coaches' conceptions of "maleness" and masculinity. For example, in a YouTube video posted by the channel of famed MMA coach, Firas Zahabi's, Tristar

Gym, Zahabi explains why he never "rolls" (i.e., grapples) with women. Zahabi explains,

> I'll tell you something. I, personally, as a trainer, as a coach, I never wrestle with
> my female students; I don't grapple with them…Now, I know some guys out
> there will be like, "Coach, I roll with women all the time and I never have an
> issue. When I roll, it's strictly jiu-jitsu. It's strictly jiu-jitsu and I never have an
> impure thought." You guys, this group of men here who say this, you guys are the
> holiest…I look up to you and I say, "These men are angelic. They're so pure of
> thought that if they roll with a beautiful, attractive girl, not the least bit of…"
> They're dead inside, let's say. I can understand if you tell me, "Coach, the girls
> are not attractive; I have no sexual thoughts." And I would say, "Look, that makes
> sense; the girl's not attractive." But, you have to understand, I can't go around
> saying, "You're ugly enough for me to roll with. No, you're too pretty." You
> wouldn't do that, right? You'd bar them all. You'd say, "Hey, look, I don't roll
> with girls…Now, for the angelic group. For you guys up there. I gotta' look at
> you up on a pedestal. You guys can roll with the most beautiful women all day
> and all night and never an impure thought enter your mind. This is how pure of
> heart you are. Me, I haven't reached this level… A girl is mounted on top of you:
> "No! Not a single impure thought has entered my mind." Come on, boys, have
> you been castrated?

Zahabi's statements demonstrate not only the persistence of the longstanding myth that

male sexual urges are "uncontrollable" and, therefore, that men's sexual aggression

against women is an outcome of biology rather than patriarchy (Jackson 2013), but also

the continued importance of heterosexuality to many MMA athletes' and coaches'

conceptions of masculinity. Consider, as well, the following statements shared by other

highly influential MMA coaches in other podcasts and on social media.

> 2 things a MAN must do!! Practice fortitude: search for overcoming obstacles,
> increasing the ability to withstand pressure, callus the mind and body. Increase the
> ability to take on the arduous. Challenges must be met daily, and with this will
> provide armor that can not be broken! Develop STRENGTH: having the ability to
> lift, move, push or pull heavy objects. Withstand forces being pushed against you,
> be able to create force against the opposition. Defend, protect the ones that look
> upon yourself to provide shelter. Don't neglect these attributes continue to grow,
> learn, evolve with honesty, open mindedness, and awareness!

Dads: We must teach our boys to be kind, but also to punch bullies in the face.
We must teach our sons to prefer peace, but also how to make war. There is still
darkness in this world, and good men are required to keep it at bay. The
responsibility to raise these MEN lies with us.

It's become encouraged now to feminize men. If they want to feminize their men,
they can do it, but they aren't going to feminize our men…The teacher was telling
my son it's okay [to be gay]. Well, that's pretty weird, man. Kids haven't even
gotten through puberty yet. I send my kid to school to math, science, history,
philosophy, ethics…the basics. Why are you showing them on Valentine's Day, a
story about a man with another man?...I tell my kids that there are gay people; you
will see them. *We* are not gay. That is what I told them, straight up, and I'm not
ashamed. I told them, "Tell your teacher you're heterosexual, and if he has a
problem with that, to call me."

Statements such as these exemplify not only the importance of a masculine identity to

men MMA athletes and coaches, but also the ubiquity of femmephobic and homophobic

ideas throughout MMA culture. This stands in stark contrast to MMA's framing as a

"progressive" sport (Channon and Matthews 2015), as well as its conception as a space of

women's empowerment.

Christianity

Like masculinity, religion occupies a very prominent place in MMA culture. And

while the athletes who compete in MMA subscribe to numerous religious faiths, the most

visible religion in MMA by far is Christianity. Several scholars have examined MMA's

relationship to Christianity (e.g., Borer and Schafer 2011; Greve 2014; Waller 2017).

Borer and Schafer (2011), for instance, examined the phenomenon of Evangelical

Christian churches incorporating MMA into their religious teachings to attract men and

boys to their services, and how Christian MMA fans reconcile the perceived conflict

between their religious beliefs and their leisure practices. Greve (2014) examined the rise

of "muscular Christianity" over the last century, as well as the commercialization of

Christianity in MMA, as evidenced by the rise of Christian MMA apparel companies like Fight 4 Christ and Jesus Didn't Tap. Waller (2017), too, discussed the embrace of MMA by Evangelical Christian churches, and how Evangelical pastors use MMA to promote "Christian" values.

The MMA community's embrace of (white, American) "Christian" ideals, such as strong male leadership, gender complementarianism, and capitalism, reinforces its vulnerability to the trappings of hegemonic masculinity and neoliberal ideology. For example, the MMA community's belief in the importance of strong male leadership and gender complementarianism reinforces men MMA athletes' desires to be seen as "leaders" and "protectors," and women MMA athletes' desires to become mothers and embrace their feminine "natures" (I will discuss this point further in Chapter 5). The MMA community's embrace of capitalism reinforces its beliefs in the importance of "individualism" and "meritocracy," as well as its rejection of socialist ideals like community, the public good, and public welfare. In this way, the (white, American) "Christian" ideals that pervade MMA culture reinforce its skepticism of social movements like feminism, #MeToo, and the Black Lives Matter movement, and further limit the sport's potential as a space of women's empowerment.

Postfeminism

Regarding the framing of women's participation in MMA, specifically, MMA culture contains many features of postfeminism (Gill 2007). These features include an emphasis on self-surveillance, monitoring, and discipline; a focus on individualism, choice, and empowerment; ideas about natural sexual difference; the hypersexualization of women's bodies; and an obsession with consumerism and the commodification of difference (Gill 2007).

The emphasis on self-surveillance, monitoring, and discipline can be observed in the daily practices of any MMA athlete. Practices like dieting, strength training, and "cutting weight" (i.e., rapid weight loss through dehydration) are requisite features of the profession, and the surveilling, monitoring, and disciplining of an MMA athlete's body are expected at all times. Women MMA athletes carry additional burdens, however, as they are assigned higher expectations for managing both their body and appearance, and performing femininity and (hetero)sexuality for their predominantly male audiences.

The focus on "individualism," "choice," and "empowerment" within MMA culture has already been discussed throughout this chapter but carries additional significance for women MMA athletes, in particular. The word, "empowerment," for example, is prominently featured throughout WMMA culture, and is commonly used to promote the consumption of WMMA fights and merchandise. A particularly interesting example comes from the Singapore-based MMA promotion, ONE Championship.

In 2021, ONE Championship held its first ever "all-women's" MMA event, aptly titled, "Empower." The event was headlined by a title fight between strawweight champion, Xiong Jing Nan, and challenger, Michelle Nicolini. The event also featured seven other women's bouts from the sports of MMA, kickboxing, and muay Thai. In the official trailer for the event, the viewer is treated to a black and white montage of various women ONE fighters coupled with an unidentified woman providing voice-over narration. In it, the narrator states,

They said I was born just to belong. They called me weak. Said I should be meek.
They said I am just a woman. But when the world refused to see me, the fire
burned within me. I told myself that nothing was impossible. And my will became
unstoppable. I am not just a woman, but a beacon of hopes and dreams. A pillar of
inspiration and strength. A fearless trailblazer. Willing to go to any length. We are
not just women. We are fighters. We are role models. We are the future.

The trailer reveals many of the trappings of postfeminist "empowerment," where the

obstacles to women's liberation are unnamed, and the process of said "empowerment" is

strictly de-politicized. Rather than calling attention to women's sexual, social, or

economic exploitation, then, or delineating the process of women's empowerment, the

video merely provides standard postfeminist tropes like, "when the world refused to see

me, the fire burned within me," and "we are the future."

The trappings of postfeminism are also revealed in ONE Championship's

recently-released "Empowered Collection" clothing line. Interestingly, while ONE chose

the word, "Empower," for the title of their first all-women's event, it is the word,

"*Empowered*," that is featured in their apparel. The message this communicates is that,

through consumption of ONE's products, women can claim empowerment for themselves

and display their empowered status. The products, ranging from "Empowered Crop Tees"

to "Empowered Crop Hoodies," feature the word, "Empowered," in big bold letters, with

the letter "O" exchanged for a pink and purple clenched fist holding a flower. The image

of the clenched fist, which has historically been used by communist, leftist, and civil

rights groups to express political resistance and solidarity, is here not only de-politicized

and stripped of its intended meaning, but also appropriated for the purpose of capitalism

and the consumption of ONE's products. In this way, ONE's leveraging of the language of "empowerment" not only reveals the influence of postfeminism, but serves to bolster one of the very forces that constrain women's autonomy.

Ideas about "natural" sexual difference are ubiquitous throughout MMA and WMMA culture. The influence of cultural figures and coaches who promote ideas of natural sexual difference in their social media and podcast content notwithstanding (e.g., Rogan, Peterson, Zahabi, etc.), the way in which women's participation in MMA is discussed by promoters, commentators, fans, and the athletes, themselves, reveals the influence of postfeminism. According to Gill (2007: 158), for a short time in the 1970s and 1980s, notions of male and female equality took hold in popular culture, but were "resolutely dispensed with" in the 1990s as they became associated with feminism and "political correctness." In addition, Gill (2007) argues, notions of sexual difference were bolstered by the explosion of self-help literature which claimed to address the question of why the "battle of the sexes" continued despite (or because of) feminism, and the repeated claim that the answer to this question was because men and women were fundamentally different (Gill 2007; see also Ward 2020). Feminism was, therefore, deemed to have lost its way when it tried to impose ideological prescriptions on a "nature" that didn't fit, and unequal power relations between men and women were "(re)eroticized" and constructed as not only "natural" and "inevitable" but also "pleasurable" (Gill 2007: 159).

Ideas of "natural" sexual difference surface almost any time an MMA promotion features women's fights. Exceedingly common is the practice of playing songs that feature the word, "girl" in preparation for women's fights—such as No Doubt's "I'm Just a Girl" or Beastie Boys' "Girls"—and, routinely, commentators will speak about women's participation in highly gendered ways, often calling attention to their roles as wives or mothers, or repeating postfeminist "Girl Power" slogans like "girls fight harder" or "fight like a girl." In fact, while attending "media day" with a member of The Mean Girls while she performed promotional labor in preparation for her first title defense, I was struck by the repeated use of the slogan, "fight like a girl," by several of the media outlets we visited. In an interview with a local news station, for example, I watched in amusement as the fighter answered questions about her participation in MMA as a woman, while the words, "fight like a girl," were prominently featured in the backdrop of the interview. I also observed her several times asked to strangle male hosts while posing for photos, in ways that were intended to call attention to the paradox of a woman strangling a man. In one such instance, the host cried out, "I'm being choked by a girl!" while the fighter strangled him from behind, causing those in attendance to erupt with laughter.

The hypersexualization of women's bodies is prominent throughout much of WMMA culture. WMMA promotional materials, such as the UFC's "Beauty and Strength" campaign, communicate that WMMA athletes' first priority is to serve the male gaze (Jennings 2015), and WMMA-inspired promotions like the Lingerie Fighting Championships (LFC) leverage the intrigue of women's scantily-clad bodies performing MMA techniques to appeal to heterosexual men's desires (Channon et al. 2018). This is also evident in the routine inclusion of ring girls at MMA events (or "Octagon Girls" in the case of the UFC), and framing of women's hypersexuality as a form of "empowerment."

The obsession with consumerism and the commodification of difference can be observed in many of the UFC's promotional materials. In fact, according to McClearen (2021), "branded difference" is an integral part of the UFC's promotional strategy. McClearen (2021: 17) defines branded difference as "the strategic efforts by the UFC to lure audiences and fighters through either meaningful or plastic representations of a variety of identities while masking the inequalities produces when difference glistens in brand culture." She further theorizes the term as a "discourse that presumes that the visibility of difference (including gender, race, sexuality, ethnicity, and nationality) in the UFC will lead to success in the ring and a stable livelihood" (McClearen 2021: 14). This presumption, McClearen (2021) argues, inspires fighters to work for the UFC even though there is limited return on the labor their visibility requires while the UFC remains the primary benefactor of their labor. At the same time, she argues, branded difference celebrates the presence and representation of women fighters in the promotion while serving as a distraction that deflects attention from the ways that visibility can hurt those same fighters. As a result, McClearen argues, the exposure that branded difference in the UFC facilitates is a "culturally and economically problematic brand strategy rather than a unilateral victory for women" (2021: 15).

WMMA POLITICS

Conservatism

The MMA community is largely right-leaning when it comes to most political and cultural issues. Indeed, there is much overlap between the MMA community's politics and those of Trump-era American conservatism. These issues include the MMA community's affinity for capitalism and hostility toward socialism and communism, their beliefs about "free speech" and the First Amendment, their affinity for guns and the Second Amendment, their affection for the U.S. military and police forces, their stances against "wokeness" and "cancel culture," their endorsement of "traditional" gender roles and hostility toward trans people, their hostility toward feminism and the Black Lives Matter movement, their endorsement of "America First" ideology and hostility toward China, their skepticism of unions, and their belief that "personal freedoms" should take precedence over the common good.

Libertarianism

Because of MMA's association with right-wing politics and neoliberal ideals like "individualism," "personal freedoms," and "personal responsibility," there is a strong affinity for cultural representations of libertarianism within MMA spaces. In fact, the Gadsden flag is commonly featured within MMA academies, and the libertarian slogan, "Don't tread on me," is routinely appropriated to sell "rash guards," fight shorts, and t-shirts within the MMA industry. This is an example of not only the MMA community's alignment with right-wing politics, but also its vulnerability to right-wing populism.

Because of MMA's framing as a "pure" form of fighting with few restrictions and limited institutional oversight, the trappings of libertarianism are particularly seductive to the MMA community. Indeed, the UFC's original slogan, "there are no rules," is remarkably consistent with libertarian ideology. And while modern MMA does indeed include rules, MMA athletes and fans alike often disparage fighters who attempt to use the rules to their advantage (such as in the case of a fighter keeping one hand on the ground to render knee strikes to the head "illegal") and routinely state that the sport would be better if it had fewer restrictions. Examples of this include popular suggestions that the sport remove the requirement of wearing gloves, bar referee intervention (most notably, in the case of referees returning athletes to the standing position after stalled action on the ground), and allow "12-to-6" elbows on the ground (i.e., elbow strikes involving the point of the elbow striking directly downward onto an opponent's head or body).

The relationship between "no holds barred" fighting and libertarianism has been discussed by other scholars. Gong (2015: 611), for example, in a study of a "no-rules" weapons fighting group, argued that his participants commonly espoused values associated with libertarianism, and understood their participation in the "no-rules" fighting group as one where "ideals of radical self-reliance and freedom from external authority can be put into practice, summed up in the often-repeated phrase, 'only you are responsible for you.'" Gong (2015) found, however, that the "no-rules" fighting participants, in fact, adhered to numerous rules and regulations which not only guided their participation but also shaped their understandings of what constituted "real" and "simulated" training. Gong (2015) argued, therefore, that even in "no-rules" fighting, rules and regulations were nevertheless central to sustaining play and generating the experience of "freedom" that fighters embraced.

The contradictions of libertarian ideology within MMA culture can be observed in the MMA community's conflicting views on bodily autonomy, as well as in their stances on numerous other social issues. While MMA athletes commonly espouse anti-vax rhetoric regarding the enforcement of COVID-19 vaccines, for example, many of these same athletes hold "pro-life" views regarding women's right to an abortion. In fact, I was struck by how few women MMA athletes, in particular, spoke out against the Supreme Court's decision to overturn Roe v. Wade, and how some have continued to publicly endorse "pro-life" politicians such as Lauren Boebert and Marjorie Taylor Greene. Other examples include the MMA community's ambivalence toward violence, with MMA fighters sometimes expressing an affinity for violence (such as in the popular expression, "Wake up and choose violence") and, other times, denouncing it. Such contradictions reveal MMA athletes' libertarian sensibilities to, in fact, be "largely patterned and predictable in accordance with the existing external rules of the civilized society in which [they are] embedded" (Gong 2015: 618) and shaped by the hypermasculine, white supremacist, and heteropatriarchal forces that pervade MMA culture.

Political Correctness and "Cancel Culture"

The MMA community is deeply skeptical of anything it perceives to be motivated by "political correctness." References to political correctness are, therefore, commonly used to deflect accusations of racism, sexism, or homophobia by MMA athletes and promoters, and maintain a white supremacist and heteropatriarchal status quo within the MMA industry. In fact, UFC president, Dana White, while defending his decision not to sanction UFC athlete, Cody Durden, for his post-fight comments at UFC Vegas 43 in which he boasted that he wanted to send his opponent, Qileng Aori, "back to China where he came from," recently explained, "In this insanely politically correct world we're living in, [the UFC] is one place that is not [politically correct]" (Butler 2021). MMA politics should, therefore, be understood, in part, through this lens.

The MMA community's hostility toward political correctness is evident in its opposition to the regulation of hate speech; its opposition to the promotion of diversity, equity, and inclusion; and its skepticism of efforts to combat various forms of inequality. MMA fighters are likewise skeptical of modern concepts like "triggers" and "microaggressions," as they understand these concepts to be manifestations of an increasingly "soft" and politically correct society. This often leads members of the MMA community to align themselves with alt-right and far-right causes—as they view alt-right and far-right figures as "rebels" in a politically correct world—and dismiss accusations of prejudice or hate speech as "overblown" or the products of liberal hysteria. A good example of this can be found in a June 2018 incident involving UFC athlete, Andrea Lee.

Lee became the subject of controversy, following her posting a photo of herself with her husband, Donny Aaron, in which the two were pictured in their swimsuits near a lake. Aaron—a former police officer who served time in prison following a 2009 conviction for negligent homicide—was pictured in the photo shirtless, revealing tattoos of a swastika and a pair of Nazi "SS" bolts on his arms. When fans called attention to the tattoos and accused Lee and her husband of racism, Lee explained that neither her nor her husband could be racists since they have "an Asian and a black guy that live with [them]," and accused fans of being "sensitive ass mofos" and instructed them to "get over [themselves]" (Samano 2018).

A similar event involved UFC athlete, Tony Kelley. Kelley, while working as a corner at UFC Vegas 54, was caught on camera referring to his fighter's opponent, Viviane Araujo, as a "dirty fucking Brazilian." When responding to accusations of racism via social media, Kelley cited "cancel culture," and explained, "Cancel Culture is real. What I said was real and in the heat of battle, and in no way had any type of racist connotations meant…but that's the way you take it, idgaf. So many people quick to say racist…that shit's getting old" (Bissell 2022). These are just two examples of the ways in which MMA athletes use accusations of "political correctness" and "cancel culture" to deflect attention away from their own behaviors and present themselves as "free thinkers" in a politically correct and uniform society.

Elective Cynicism

MMA athletes are deeply cynical about many institutions in society, including politics, news media, science, education, and law. Believing such institutions to be morally bankrupt, MMA athletes commonly express a distrust in these institutions and present themselves as morally and intellectually superior to those who adhere to them (see also Abramson and Modzelewski [2011] for a discussion of MMA fighters' self-conceptions as morally superior). To characterize MMA athletes as merely cynical, however, would miss the point that it is an *elective* cynicism to which they subscribe—

manifested, at best, unevenly and in ways that reveal the underlying beliefs that guide their actions and behaviors. While MMA athletes routinely express a cynical view of liberal politicians, "the media," and "the medical establishment," for example, they also express a surprising degree of trust in conservative politicians, "alternative media," and alternative health practitioners, as well as documented liars and scam artists like Alex Jones, Tucker Carlson, and Andrew Tate. I, therefore, use the term, *elective cynicism*, to describe MMA athletes' anti-institutional sensibilities and capture the contradictory ways in which they are expressed.

Freedom Fight Night

Perhaps, never have the politics of MMA been on display more proudly than in the March 2022 MMA event, "Freedom Fight Night" (FFN). FFN was founded by the self-proclaimed "anti-woke CEO," Harrison Rogers, and was marketed as an explicitly conservative MMA event. According to FFN's website, Rogers—a lifelong MMA fan— founded FFN after he began to see "America's freedom's [sic] being challenged and slipping away" (FreedomFightNight.com). Rogers, therefore, set out to create an explicitly conservative MMA promotion to counter what he saw as a left-wing bias in professional sports. The event culminated in a bizarre mix of regional MMA action and conservative propaganda, and exemplified many of the political proclivities of MMA athletes and culture.

Serving as commentators for FFN were stand-up comedian, Bryan Lacey, and former UFC champion, Frank Mir. As the event's broadcast commenced, Lacey was first to address the broadcast audience. He began,

Good evening, ladies and gentlemen, I'm Bryan Lacey. Welcome to Freedom Fight Night. Alongside me, a legend of the game, a man who would surely have his face painted on the Mt. Rushmore of MMA, Mr. Frank Mir. Frank, a pleasure to be here. What a night this is set to be. I mean, this is not just about the fights though, right? This is about something deeper than that and something that is very close to your heart. Tell us a bit about it.

A seemingly intoxicated Mir, smiling from ear to ear, then responded,

As I've gotten older, I wanna' give back to the U.S. And how can I make my country stronger? How can I make…and I've realized it's our youth. And, right now, we're in a culture war that we are losing. The Left owns Hollywood, they own higher education, our big major sporting teams are Left influences, and then when our children grow up to admire these athletes and actresses, they admire all their concepts. So, what I've seen with our travels throughout the country or throughout the world is I see youths in other countries admire warriors. They admire doctors. They admire wrestlers in the Olympics. They admire *fighters*. And so, our warriors weren't allowed a platform to discuss these things, so that's why I'm happy that CloutHub were able to showcase that tonight and were able to talk and discuss…and, again, this is the identity I wanna' give our youth. I wanna' give them the fact that we're gonna' win this culture war, show our young men and women that there are people that think conservatively, and that are like-minded warriors out here and establish that platform.

As the night progressed, the broadcast audience was treated to many more exchanges like this, complete with monologues about "cancel culture," "law enforcement," and "being a warrior."

Among the many things that distinguished FFN from other MMA events, were its pre-recorded segments dedicated to contemporary social issues which aired between bouts. Presented under the title, "Issue Focus," these segments included carefully crafted statements by Mir and Rogers. The topics, or "issue foci," included "Supporting Public Safety," "Smaller Government," "Individual Rights," "American Strength," and "Educational Choice." For example, in the segment titled, "Individual Rights," Rogers stated,

America's founding was based on the principles of independence and individual rights. But today's leaders are threatening individual rights in our country more than we've ever seen in modern history. From personal medical mandates to them trying to force our companies to fine or even fire their employees, power means everything and individual rights mean nothing. We must get back to the core principles of America. Individual rights matter. The Constitution matters. Freedom *matters*.

In another segment, titled, "American Strength," Mir stated,

Peace through strength was the cornerstone of President Ronald Reagan's foreign policy. And his projection of American strength was so successful, it led to the end of a forty-year Cold War and brought freedom to millions across the world. Sadly, we can see the alarming consequences of projecting American weakness today: global instability and war. If we're going to succeed in expanding freedom, we need leaders who will recommit us to the idea of peace through strength.

Such segments stood out as, perhaps, the most overt form of political propaganda ever featured in an MMA broadcast and exemplified MMA's increasingly visible role in the American "culture wars" (Borer and Schafer 2011).

WMMA SUBJECTHOOD

Neoliberal-Postfeminist Subjects

WMMA athletes represent the quintessential neoliberal-postfeminist subjects. Their lives are characterized by a continuous process of self-discipline, -surveillance, and -cultivation, as well as a constant state of precarity in an entrepreneurial labor market that grants monopolistic power to the UFC and little to no bargaining power to the athletes who sustain it. Most of these athletes work full- or part-time jobs in addition to MMA— because they are unable to sustain themselves on income produced through MMA competition alone—and increasingly these athletes are supplementing their incomes with money earned through subscription-based websites, such as OnlyFans.com, by selling nude and/or semi-nude photos (or by selling previously-worn intimate items such as used socks or underwear).

Many of these athletes subscribe to postfeminist ideas of empowerment through choice, liberalism, and meritocracy—while being paid less than their male counterparts—and advocate conservative gender ideals, even while being celebrated for their own gender transgressions. To these athletes, individual success is privileged above all else, and little effort is made to distance themselves from the perception of them as self-interested, neoliberal entrepreneurs. Indeed, a common talking point among WMMA athletes is the repeated claim that MMA is a "selfish sport." This talking point, in fact, presented itself many times throughout my interviews.

> Fighting's such a selfish sport. . .so selfish. I've put that before my relationships. That's how selfish it is. (Maria, 29, Latina, straight)

> You have to be selfish. Fighting is a very selfish sport. (Kani, 22, white, straight)

> I think fighting is a very selfish sport. (Autumn, 28, white, straight)

While the word "selfish" typically carries negative connotations, WMMA athletes reclaim selfishness as an essential feature of their profession. This exempts them from feelings of shame or guilt as it reframes their own self-serving behaviors as requisite for success in a hypercompetitive sport. This also coincides with a lack of prosocial behaviors, more generally, and is compounded by a postfeminist sensibility (Gill 2007) that understands women to occupy an innate gendered disposition that is inherently hostile toward other women. This is evidenced by the common claim that WMMA athletes fight "harder" and "more emotionally," and that, for them, the fight is more "personal" than it is for their male counterparts. The head coach of The Mean Girls actually commodified this trope into a shirt, which he sells on his social media profiles, with the words, "The Broadfather," on the front—an allusion to his role as the head coach of a professional WMMA team—and "Girls can't get along anyway so they might as well fight each other for money," on the back. Although the quote is meant to be humorous, it, in fact, accurately reflects the social reality of the sport, in which there is a distinct lack of solidarity between the women entrepreneurs who occupy it.

It is important to emphasize, however, that this lack of solidarity is not innate to the athletes, themselves, but rather reflects the ideologies that govern the sport. Cultural influencers like Rogan, Peterson, and Willink, routinely promote neoliberal ideals of personal responsibility and individualism, and portray feminists and activists as misguided "social justice warriors," influencing the perception of feminist efforts within the sport as unpopular and undesirable. Promoters such as UFC President, Dana White, further erode athlete solidarity by routinely matching up teammates against one another and lambasting any athletes who express reluctance to fight teammates as unserious. This all comes at a particular cost to women MMA athletes, who are both underpaid and underpromoted (see McClearen 2021) and are left without a political framework through which to interpret their unequal treatment.

Feminism

Other postfeminist sentiments to which WMMA athletes subscribe were revealed through discussions of feminism throughout my interviews. Gill (2007) argues that because postfeminism includes the double entanglement of both feminist and antifeminist ideals, antifeminist talking points are common among young women who understand feminism to be a restrictive, coercive practice that is both undesirable and unnecessary in their daily lives. Many of the athletes I interviewed made efforts to distance themselves from feminists and "the feminist agenda," despite not actually being asked any questions about feminism. For instance, when discussing WMMA as a site of empowerment, Alice (27, white, straight) clarified, "I wouldn't call myself a feminist or anything. I don't believe I am in most modern terminology." When asked to elaborate, she continued,

> Like, with the military, I feel like if a woman can compete and do everything that a man can do without the test being changed, great, let her do whatever the job entails. But, if they have to change the test so that she can pass, I don't like that. That doesn't make me feel empowered. That makes me feel like they had to dumb it down for you. But some women want it dumbed down so that they can have the same status. And I'm not against us having the same status but earn it just like everyone else.

Kate (28, white, straight), a former member of the United States military, expressed similar sentiments, explaining,

> I don't like feminists—the feminist agenda…I don't have to march and get crazy; I just *do*. I've never not been able to do whatever I wanted to do because of my gender, besides serving in an infantry role because at the time women weren't allowed to…that's not what I wanted to do anyway. I'm more of an empowerment type. And that goes for both genders. Do whatever you want. It's super easy.

Some of the athletes explained that they were unsupportive of feminism because they felt women should have to "prove themselves," reflecting Rottenberg's (2018, 195) claim that the colonization of neoliberalism and postfeminism has produced a "very clear distinction between worthy 'aspirational' female subjects and the majority of female subjects who are deemed irredeemable due to their insufficient aspiration and thus 'responsibilization.'" Others argued that their lack of support of feminism was due to their belief that women were not only not disadvantaged in society but were actually privileged.

> I actually think that now, like currently, that it's harder for white males than anybody. Women complain about not having this, not having that, and how it's not fair and it's so much harder to be a woman. There was a time, but I think now we're finally to the point where women complain about it more than it's actually really true. I mean if you get pulled over by a cop and I get pulled over by a cop and I start crying like, "I didn't mean to! I'm sorry!" Who's gonna' get let off? It's not gonna' be you, it's gonna' be me. (Megan, 31, white, straight)

Such statements obscure the very real inequities that exist between and within genders, as well as between and within races, classes, and other social groups. Although neoliberal-postfeminist logics reduce any such inequities to the result of individual poor choices and/or a lack of hard work and investment in the self (Gill 2007), these logics are refuted by a wealth of sociological research that has long documented the ways in which such inequities have been shaped and maintained by social structures that privilege white, heterosexual men in particular. Such contradictions are an essential feature of neoliberal–postfeminist subjecthood, however (Banet-Weiser, Gill, and Rottenberg 2020), as neoliberal–postfeminist logics are unequipped to reconcile the discontinuity between a worldview that fails to recognize structural inequality and a material world that continues to be shaped by it. This subjecthood defines the prototypical WMMA athlete who, in their entrepreneurial pursuits in a white male-dominated sport, is often supportive of the very ideologies that maintain their unequal status.

Empowerment

To better understand whether the athletes in my study experienced MMA as a space of empowerment, I asked them whether they considered themselves empowered, and, if so, what that meant to them. While most of the athletes did consider themselves

empowered, interestingly, many of these athletes constructed their empowered status in

relation to other *women*. For example, Autumn (29, white, straight) revealed that, for her,

being empowered meant "doing stuff that other women would be afraid to do." Similarly,

Kristina (30, Mixed, straight) revealed that she considers herself empowered because she

is more mentally and emotionally capable than "your average woman." Others even

included criticisms of women in their conceptions of empowerment, constructing their

empowered status in relation to these women's weaknesses.

> I don't need the same things I see other women need or lean on because I have my
> own strength. (Nicole, 53, white, straight)

> I've just known a lot of weak females…so I'm not on that spectrum. (Aubrey, 27,
> white, lesbian)

References to female weakness were also made when discussing women's lack of

participation in combat sports. For example, when asked why more women do not

participate in combat sports, Kate (28, white, straight) explained,

> Because they're pussies! It hurts, and it's hard. There's a mental
> factor…Anybody can go in there and train Zumba. You go in there and you're
> moving around and flailing your arms. But you start picking apart people and they
> fold. They'd rather just continue what they're doing. They'd rather just have kids.

Other athletes cited "intimidation" as the main reason more women do not

participate in combat sports, such as Madelyn (29, white, straight), who explained that "it

takes a certain type of girl to stay with it." References such as these to a "certain type of

girl" were commonly used by the athletes to distinguish themselves from "regular"

women, against whom they defined themselves as exceptional. For instance, Kani (22, white, straight) explained, "A girl like me and other girls who started at a young age, it's all we've known. But, a *regular* female, they're like, 'I'll never be able to do that.'"

These perceived shortcomings of "regular" women were also quickly reduced to biology, and further reflected essentialized postfeminist notions of "natural" sexual difference (Gill 2007). For example, Kelly (39, white, straight) explained, "In general, and I know this is stereotyping here but…I think women were designed to be softer. That's why we carry children. And, so, I don't think that every single woman has that aggression in her that needs an expression in that way." Likewise, Allison (24, Latina, straight) explained,

> I think most girls just physically and mentally. . .I'm all for women—girl power all the way—but it's not in our DNA to be physical or competitive necessarily. Even with animals, the females, for the most part, don't hunt. They stay home, take care of the kids, and I think that's just how it is in our DNA for whatever reason.

Leilani (28, Hawaiian, straight) expressed a similar sentiment in explaining how women were not "wired" for combat, as did Jasmine (27, Asian, straight) who explained that, "evolutionarily," men were just more aggressive and better equipped to handle the rigors of combat sports. She continued,

> Of course, you get those outliers but, in general, fighting and being aggressive and getting hurt, biologically, is something that, in most species, the males do. You can do whatever you want but there's still like that separation of the sexes where the woman is more likely to do this other thing and fighting is not that other thing.

Physical Feminism

These references to biology also presented themselves in conversations about the athletes' ability to defend themselves against male violence. Although several scholars have engaged with McCaughey's (1997) "physical feminism" theory in analyzing women's combat sports (e.g., Channon and Phipps 2017; Quinney 2016; Velija, Mierzwinski, and Fortune 2013), offering support for the claim that through physical training, "what is usually taken for granted as a fact of nature—that a woman simply cannot physically challenge a man—is revealed as a social script which privileges men at the expense of women" (McCaughey 1997: 8), many of the athletes in this study did not actually think they were capable of physically defending themselves against men. For example, Leilani (28, Hawaiian, straight) explained, "Even though I'm a pro fighter…the reality of it is that I would totally be overpowered by a guy—even if he doesn't have any training." Similarly, Kani (22, white, straight) explained,

> I know I'm a badass, but in the female division. I'm sorry but if a man ran up on me, I'm going to do my 100 percent best to try to defend myself. . . but, there's just a different strength between a man and a woman. . .there's girls in my fights that can take my punches in the first minute and not go down; what do you think a man's gonna do? I know I cannot beat up a man.

Some of the athletes cited their experiences grappling with men as "proof" that differences in male and female biology would leave them unequipped to deal with men's physical size and strength. For example, Paige (31, Latina, straight) recalled instances of wrestling with her husband as evidence of the limits of female strength.

> My husband's a bigger man and we wrestle all the time and play-fight and I'll put him in an armbar, for instance, and he will pick me up with that one arm and lift me straight in the air. And I'm like, "Oh, God, this doesn't work." Or, once he starts to use his strength, he'll hold me down and I can't move. . .and also my experiences in the gym with dudes that are bigger and stronger, it doesn't matter how skilled they are. If they can hold me down, I'm not moving.

Similarly, Gabriella (30, white, straight) explained that, although she used to believe in men and women's equality, training with men has revealed to her the differences in men and women's physical abilities.

> I used to be like "men and women are super equal" and thought that all growing
> up. My mom was a very strong woman—single mom, raised my sister and me,
> and we were both like, "I can do anything." I still have that mentality a lot, but
> I've also been humbled a lot because I've trained with a man with a smaller
> structure than me in the same weight class and they hit so much harder than a
> woman. And I've felt those differences between the sexes and there are definitely
> physical differences between a man and a woman.

As Gabriella recalls her experiences training with male athletes, she depicts a journey from feminist naïveté to the "enlightened" standpoint of a WMMA athlete who experiences the "reality" of sexual difference in her daily training. Statements like these are not unique to this sample of WMMA athletes but are rather reflective of those expressed by other WMMA athletes throughout MMA media. For example, when asked about what it's like to train with her male teammates, a former UFC title challenger explained,

> I fully know that men are stronger than women—I'm not delusional, *I'm not some
> feminist*—even though I might be taller or weigh more than some of them,
> physically, I'm not as strong as them. But it makes me better because, if I can
> hold my own against guys who are stronger or bigger than me, then when I go
> into a cage with a female my own size or weighing a little less, they don't feel
> *half* of what I've dealt with in the gym. (Helwani 2018, emphasis added)

Such statements highlight a clear difference between the experiences of WMMA athletes and those of the women's self-defense students in McCaughey's (1997) study; although WMMA athletes undoubtedly acquire impressive physical skills that leave them better equipped to defend themselves against male violence, because their training is not accompanied by the development of a critical consciousness, these athletes are nevertheless unable to challenge patriarchal scripts of female vulnerability and male superiority. Rather, it seems, these athletes' experiences of training with men only serve to concretize their beliefs in male superiority and allow them to justify gender inequality.

The Breaking Barriers Paradox

The confluence of neoliberalism and postfeminism in the context of women's empowerment sets the stage for what I term, "the breaking barriers paradox." I propose this term to characterize the ways in which women's achievements (in MMA and elsewhere) are framed as both a source of women's empowerment and a celebration of women's liberation. Reminiscent of the "Girl Power" discourse of the 1990s (Gill and Scharff 2013), "breaking barriers" discourse recasts women's inequality and exploitation as symbols of women's unique (and "natural") strength, power, and resilience in a world which no longer needs feminist intervention, and in the process recasts feminist calls for empowerment as celebrations of women's *empowered*-ment. Rather than being used to call attention to the social and economic barriers that render women's empowerment necessary, then, "breaking barriers" discourse holds women's achievements up as symbols of women's "progress" and "liberation."

The breaking barriers paradox is at once a celebration of human agency over social structure and at the same time a denial of the existence of the very structure it claims to be overcoming. Rather than being used to call attention to the harms of capitalism, white supremacy, or heteropatriarchy, then, "breaking barriers" discourse suggests that the *real* barrier to women's empowerment is women, themselves (e.g., "the only one who can prevent you from achieving your goals is *you*"). In this way, the "barrier breaker" is used as a symbol of women's empowerment who calls on her unique "inner strength" to overcome obstacles through "hard work," "determination," and "will power," rather than "being a victim" or "asking for a handout." This preserves the patriarchal status quo and maintains a system of inequality and exploitation that is not only experienced by women in MMA but women around the world.

Examples of the breaking barriers paradox can be found in many of the social media posts authored by WMMA athletes. For example, on International Women's Day (and throughout Women's History Month in the United States), many WMMA athletes take to social media to post statements about women's empowerment and its relationship to women's MMA. But rather than using these posts to call attention to gender inequities or the need to elevate women's status in society, these posts are more commonly used to celebrate women's unique "natural" power and the "barriers" women have already overcome. For example, here are a few of the posts published by WMMA athletes for International Women's Day 2021.

> Smile, it is #internationalwomensday. Here's to all the challenges, biases, and barriers we have overcome.

> Be brave. Be beautiful. Be strong. Be a mom. Be a warrior. Be a trailblazer. Be whatever makes you feel like the amazing woman you are! Cheers to all the badass women out there. Happy International Women's Day…and thank you the equally amazing men who recognize the strength of the women in their life. What is the quality you most admire about the woman closest to you? Tag her and let her know!!!

> Happy International Women's Day. Thank you @prettylittlething for choosing me to host this year's event. As a woman in a male dominated industry, I continuously push myself to break barriers and inspire others. I have constantly had people diminish me, doubt me, and tell me I need to look a certain way in order to be successful in my career. But through it all, I have stayed true to who I am, and believed in myself and my message more than anything. I believe you can be glamorous and feminine, and still be a bad ass in the cage, or in whatever you do in life. So, ladies, let's come together and show the world we can be BOTH strong and beautiful!

> I am tough. I am resilient. I can hold a child's hand and soothe a baby. I can bring a man to his knees. I am sexy. I can be soft and sweet or bold and harsh. I am

independent. My body is beautiful. I have curves, I have scars. My small body can move mountains. I am pretty but I will get dirty. I am a woman. I will stand up for other women. I will not ever back down. We will never back down. #internationalwomensday

Happy International Women's Day to all of the strong women holding it down! Whether you chose a career or to stay at home caring for your family, whether you choose to wear pant suits or show a little skin, I feel grateful that we are in a time when we can CHOOSE to do anything we want and be anyone we want!

Fix those crowns, ladies. Love the skin you're in, trust your instincts, hustle hard, speak your mind, and don't take sh*t from anybody! Happy International Women's Day!

I am a woman, born and raised. I am honored to say that I've birthed two wonderful humans. I'm honored to say I am a 2x World Champion fighter, Pan American Champion along with other @ibjjf Open gold medals. I'm a business owner, and wife. If there's any doubt in you at all that being a woman, that you are for whatever reason at a disadvantage- YOU are wrong. Being a woman makes you infinitely more powerful. Keep shining ladies because no one will rain on this parade.

It's always amazing to remember how strong and powerful women are. Fight like a girl. #internationalwomensday

Something people don't know about me is that growing up I always wanted to be a boy bc I noticed how they were treated differently. My brother got to stay out later, was allowed to stay the night at his friends' houses, played cooler sports, was stronger than me. I even went as far as dressing like a boy and doing things boys did. I even kissed a girl once. Boy…was I wrong. Being a woman is way more cool. The older I get, the more I embrace my feminine grace while still being able to kick some fucking ass. Girls rule. Happy Women's Day to all the women in the world.

Consistent among these posts is the celebration of women's unique "natural" qualities

(e.g., femininity, beauty, and strength), as well as women's unique ability to "overcome"

barriers. Also consistent among these posts, however, is the naturalization of such

barriers and their framing as inevitable features of society rather than patriarchy. Rather

than calling attention to the need to dismantle these barriers, then, "breaking barriers" discourse, paradoxically, frames such barriers as resources for harnessing women's unique strength, resilience, and power. In the process, gender inequities are de-problematized and patriarchy is rendered "normal," if not desirable.

CONCLUSION

In this chapter, I have shown how MMA culture is shaped by the influences of neoliberalism, postfeminism, wellness, masculinity, and Christianity. I have also shown how MMA politics are distinctly right-wing and shaped by (white, American) conservative and libertarian ideals. Finally, I have shown how these influences shape WMMA subjecthood and influence WMMA athletes' self-conceptions as self-interested, neoliberal entrepreneurs.

I have also demonstrated how WMMA athletes' adherence to neoliberal-postfeminist logics obscures their understanding of empowerment and encourages their individual-centric worldviews. Rather than understanding empowerment as a process through which women challenge patriarchal ideology; transform the structures and institutions that reinforce and perpetuate gender discrimination and social inequality; and enable women to gain greater access to, and control of, material and informational resources (Batliwala 1994); WMMA athletes understand empowerment as an individualized "journey" in the pursuit of human capital (Cornwall 2016; Radhakrishnan and Solari 2022). Rather than using their platforms to critique the structures of capitalism, white supremacy, and heteropatriarchy that constrain women's lives, then, WMMA athletes, paradoxically, appropriate feminist calls for empowerment to reinforce capitalist, white supremacist, and heteropatriarchal ideals. This is not only inconsistent with feminist theorizing of empowerment, but directly antithetical to it.

Regarding WMMA's potential as a site of "physical feminism" (McCaughey 1997), my interviews revealed stark differences between WMMA athletes and the "self-defensers" in McCaughey's (1997) study. Rather than demonstrating an awareness of the ways in which women's perceived vulnerability and lack of physical power have been shaped by social, cultural, and historical forces, the athletes in my sample demonstrated a strong belief in the "nature" of male superiority, as well as a distinct lack of awareness of the social forces that shape women's experiences. Rather than using their participation in MMA to challenge the "rape myths" that reinforce the belief that women need protection from bad men by good men (Burke 2019; McCaughey 1997), then, the athletes in my study failed to question these narratives and even made statements that reinforced them.

Finally, in this chapter, I have introduced an original concept, "the breaking barriers paradox," to conceptualize the ways in which women's achievements are framed as both a source of women's empowerment and a celebration of women's liberation. At once, a celebration of human agency over social structure and, at the same time, a denial of the existence of the very structure it claims to be overcoming, I have shown how "breaking barriers" discourse serves to obscure the processes of women's *structural* empowerment and strengthen the very structures that constrain women's autonomy. Rather than calling attention to the harms of these structures, "breaking barriers" discourse perpetuates neoliberal-postfeminist appropriations of women's empowerment to advance neoliberal capitalist, white supremacist, and heteropatriarchal ideology. In this way, the "barrier breaker" is held up as a source of motivation for women to aspire toward as they call on their unique "inner strength" on their path toward empowerment, as well as a symbol of women's unique "natural" strength, resilience, and power in a world which no longer needs feminist intervention. Through this process, feminist conceptions of empowerment are rendered unintelligible, and neoliberal-postfeminist notions of *empowered*-ment are installed in their place.

CHAPTER IV: #GETYOUAGIRLTHATCANDOBOTH: THE FEMALE-ATHLETE COMMODITY AND THE DOING AND SELLING OF GENDER IN WMMA

In January of 2021, I started to see videos on social media of WMMA athletes participating in a women's "empowerment" campaign alongside the hashtag, "#GetYouAGirlThatCanDoBoth." The campaign featured short videos of several high-profile WMMA athletes in their professional fight gear spliced together with videos of these same athletes in stereotypically feminine attire, such as dresses, high-heeled shoes, and makeup. The purpose of the campaign was to emphasize the duality of WMMA fighters' woman-athlete subjectivities and show that women fighters could be "both" athletic and feminine. Seemingly, the campaign was also intended to inspire other women athletes to do the same and demonstrate that their participation in sport does not have to come at the expense of their femininity.

Another interpretation of this campaign, however, is to show that WMMA athletes can do "both" *masculinity* and femininity. Rather than demonstrating that MMA can be de-gendered and disassociated from masculinity, then, women's embodiment of MMA is juxtaposed against women's embodiment of femininity to emphasize, paradoxically, how distinctly *masculine* the behaviors associated with MMA are. By emphasizing the "paradox" of their participation in the "masculine" sport of MMA, however, women fighters are able to market themselves as "exceptional" women who have the power to "do both," and emphasize their value as female-athlete commodities.

In this chapter, I take seriously this notion of "doing both" and discuss its relationship to "doing gender" (West and Zimmerman 1987). I argue that "doing both" represents a novel form of gender commodification that allows (some) women athletes to capitalize on the perceived paradox of their participation in "masculine" sport by juxtaposing traditional aspects of masculinity and femininity. I caution, however, that such an approach reproduces the gender binary and reaffirms patriarchal gender hierarchies. Rather than a site for "undoing gender" (Deutsch 2007; Risman 2009), then, I argue that WMMA is a space where conservative gender ideals are pervasive, and rigid standards of masculinity and femininity reign supreme.

INTRODUCTION

Recent scholarship on women in combat sports has devoted substantial attention to the arena of martial arts and combat sports (MACS) as a space for women to challenge gender norms and construct new femininities (e.g., Channon 2014; Channon and Phipps 2017; Davies and Deckert 2018; Maclean 2016; Noel 2009; Quinney 2016; Weaving 2014). Channon, in particular, has been instrumental in identifying MACS spaces as sites for "undoing gender" (Deutsch 2007; Risman 2009) and reshaping gender attitudes. Maclean (2016) argues that such spaces foster relations that subvert "traditional" gender norms, as well as gender ideals and hierarchies, while Davies and Deckert (2018: 15) argue that these spaces allow women participants to "appropriate male symbols of physical capital and shift gender relations of power." According to Channon and Phipps (2017: 27), these spaces may even allow women to develop new femininities that are "intelligible as feminine but work against the maintenance of male hegemony."

Yet research on WMMA suggests that the arena of MACS is also a space where gender is heavily policed, and even sanctioned (Weaving 2014; Jennings 2015;

McClearen 2015). Jennings (2014), for example, described how former UFC women's bantamweight champion, Cris Cyborg, was routinely accused of being "too masculine" by fans and observers, and even accused of being a man. McClearen (2015: 74) examined the treatment of transgender fighter, Fallon Fox, and showed how Fox was routinely subject to transphobic harassment, and how the discourse surrounding Fox's participation in MMA reaffirmed a "patriarchal, cisgender, cissexual system of power by exaggerating 'biologically' sanctioned male physical dominance and 'innate' female physical lack." While scholars have been optimistic about the gender-transgressive potential of MACS, is this potential currently being realized in WMMA?

In this chapter, I discuss the rise of what I term, "the female-athlete commodity," and its relationship to WMMA athletes' desires to "do both." I begin by outlining the sociology of sport literature on women athletes before discussing women athletes' relationship to social media. I then discuss the doing and selling of gender in WMMA and explicate my original concepts, "the female-athlete commodity" and "doing both." Finally, I discuss the potential of "doing both" in men's MMA, as well as in other gendered arenas.

THE FEMALE-ATHLETE PARADOX

The Apologetic

Research in the sociology of sport has illuminated the complex and often contradictory position of women athletes in patriarchal societies. Much of this research has centered around the perceived incongruity of femininity and athleticism—the so-called "female-athlete paradox" (Felshin 1974)—that female athletes must negotiate in order to be intelligible as heterofeminine women while participating in "masculine"

sports (e.g., Ezzell 2009; George 2005; Krane et al. 2004; Macro, Viveiros, and Cipriano

2009; Mennesson 2000). Because Western society emphasizes a feminine body and

demeanor, marked by smallness, vulnerability, and submissiveness, while sport

emphasizes an athletic body and demeanor, marked by strength, fitness, and aggression,

women athletes face competing expectations from sport and society, causing frustration

and anxiety for many of these athletes (Clasen 2001; Krane et al. 2004). The presence of

this paradox has been discussed in numerous women's sports, including soccer (Kassing

2018), basketball (Bennett et al. 2017), and boxing (Lafferty and McCay 2004;

Mennesson 2000), as well as others.

Investigations into this paradox have revealed that women athletes in many sports

engage in impression management strategies to maintain a feminine identity, such as the

tendency for these women to "apologize" (Felshin 1974) for their athleticism by

emphasizing their femininity and heterosexuality, and demonstrating that they are

"women first, athletes second" (Heywood and Dworkin 2003: 26). As articulated by

Felshin (1974: 37),

> The woman athlete must document the validity of her womanhood within the
> cultural connotations of femininity. To do this, she frequently denies the
> importance of her athletic endeavors and avows the importance of her appearance
> and the desire to be attractive and to marry and raise a family as the overriding
> motivations of her life.

This "apologetic" (Felshin 1974) involves a wide range of behaviors, including

emphasizing a heterofeminine appearance, associating with male intimate partners,

avoiding association with lesbian or masculine women, advocating conservative gender ideals, downplaying physical strength and athleticism, and emphasizing the superiority of

male athletes (Davis-Delano, Pollock, and Ellsworth Vose 2009). Such behaviors have

been observed in a wide range of women's sports (e.g., Adams, Schmitke, and Franklin

2009; Blinde and Taub 1992; Davis-Delano, Pollock, and Ellsworth Vose 2009; George

2005; Mennesson 2000), as women athletes who engage in these behaviors are rewarded

psychologically, socially, and materially for cultivating physical and behavioral

difference from men (McCaughey 1997).

The Unapologetic, The Reformed Apologetic, and Heterosexy-Fit

Recently, however, scholars have begun to question the extent to which women

athletes are "apologizing" for their participation in "masculine" sports, or experiencing

their sports participation as a threat to their femininity. Macro et al. (2009), for example,

reported that the women wrestlers in their study did not engage in behaviors consistent

with the "apologetic," nor did they experience conflict between their identities as women

and athletes. Similarly, Hardy (2015) reported that the women rugby players in her study

did not engage in "apologetic" behavior, despite being surrounded by media images that

promoted it. In an earlier study, Broad (2001: 181) even argued that the women rugby

players in her study engaged in "unapologetic" behavior—comprised of "transgressing

gender, destabilizing the heterosexual/homosexual binary, and 'in your face'

confrontations of stigma"—which she theorized as a form of "queer resistance."

Ezzell (2009) observed that, while the women rugby players in his study reported

that they did not experience their participation in rugby as a threat to their femininity,

they nevertheless demonstrated behaviors consistent with the "apologetic," such as emphasizing their femininity and heterosexuality and emphasizing the superiority of male athletes. Ezzell (2009), therefore, proposed the term, "heterosexy-fit," to describe women athletes' desires to perform traditional aspects of femininity and heterosexuality, despite their insistence that their sport participation was unthreatening to their statuses as heterofeminine women. Ezzell (2009: 112) described this "heterosexy-fit" identity as "simultaneously tough, fit, feminine, and heterosexual" and framed it as an "updated version" of emphasized femininity (Connell 1987). Consistent with Felshin's (1974) concept of "the apologetic," Ezzell (2009: 111) contended that the "heterosexy-fit" identity, while displaying some traits inconsistent with "traditional" femininity, "ultimately reinforced heterosexism and gender inequality."

Other scholars have adopted the term, "reformed apologetic" (Festle 1996), to describe women athletes' desires to emphasize their femininity and heterosexuality without diminishing their athleticism (Macro, Viveiros, and Cipriano 2009; Malcom 2003; Royce, Gebelt, and Duff 2003). Understanding this as an outcome of the greater acceptance of women's athleticism over time, scholars have argued that the "reformed" apologetic is more common among women athletes today (Macro, Viveiros, and Cipriano 2009; Malcom 2003). As explained by Malcom 2003: 1387),

> As a result of women's greater participation in sport and society's concomitant growing acceptance of female athleticism, female athletes no longer downplay the traditionally masculine traits of aggression and toughness as they relate to the athletic competition. However, they continue to overemphasize traditionally feminine traits. Theberge (2000) reinforces this assertion, suggesting that although it is no longer unacceptable for women to be successful athletes, it remains imperative that they also be appropriately feminine. Thus, female athletes employ the "reformed" apologetic defense, exaggerating their femininity while at the same time embracing their athleticism.

While women athletes, therefore, continue to "do" gender (West and Zimmerman 1987) in ways that emphasize their statuses as heterofeminine women, they simultaneously appear increasingly comfortable embracing their athleticism, as well as traits consistent with "traditional" aspects of masculinity, such as aggression and toughness.

Social Media

An important development in the doing of gender in women's sports has been the advent of social media. Because traditional media, to the extent that they have covered women athletes at all, have historically presented women athletes in sexualized, marginalized, and objectified ways (Bruce 2015; Cooky, Messner, and Hextrum 2013), social media has been theorized as a potential tool for women athletes to redress their lack of coverage, and contest normative categories of gender and sexuality in sport (Antunovic and Hardin 2012; Toffoletti and Thorpe 2018). Accordingly, contemporary analyses of women's sports have increasingly considered the role of social media in shaping women athletes' gender performances (e.g., Geurin-Eagleman and Burch 2016; Kassing 2018; Thorpe, Toffoletti, and Bruce 2017; Toffoletti and Thorpe 2018; Xu and Armstrong 2019).

Toffoletti and Thorpe (2018: 12) argue, however, that, despite social media's potential to challenge dominant representational regimes by providing avenues for women athletes to enhance their visibility on their own terms, social media has done little to alter the hegemonic gender ideals that pervade women's sports. Rather, they argue that women athletes are adopting new strategies for identity construction that capitalize on tropes of agentic postfeminist subjecthood—such as "self-love" and "self-empowerment"—in ways that ultimately reproduce gender binaries and hierarchies. They

also argue that women athletes with the largest social media followings tend to be those

who do not explicitly challenge gender norms or the associations between maleness and

sport, and instead display a "sporty and heterosexy, fashionable femininity" (Toffoletti

and Thorpe 2018: 20). They also caution that,

> The representation of sportswomen is being reconfigured under neoliberalism to
> place increased responsibility on female athletes themselves to generate social
> media coverage, broadcast a successful image of female athleticism and establish
> themselves as a unique sporting brand in highly competitive markets and
> neoliberal economies (Toffoletti and Thorpe 2018: 28-29).

McClearen (2021), in her analysis of women in the UFC, considered the role of

social media in shaping WMMA athletes' gender performances. She argued that fighters

in the UFC are forced to compete for attention in a neoliberal "economy of visibility"

(Banet-Weiser 2015) that adopts,

> [t]he meritocratic approach that if a fighter works hard enough at MMA and at
> self-promotion online, then they will prove themselves worthy of financial
> rewards. If visibility fails to materialize, neoliberal logics fault the individual
> fighter rather than the promotion, which in turn allows the UFC to refuse to
> promote its fighters without demonstrated fan engagement. Invisibility becomes a
> fighter's challenge to overcome rather than a series of cultural and economic
> conditions that dictate where the light of visibility shines (McClearen 2021: 110).

As McClearen (2021, 28) explained, however, within this economy of visibility, there is a

"hierarchy of visibility" that privileges hegemonic masculinity and emphasized

femininity over queerness, and whiteness over all other races. McClearen (2021), argued,

therefore, that WMMA athletes are incentivized to adopt a hyperfeminine, heterosexy

image and appeal to a conventional straight male gaze in order to advance their MMA

careers.

The Female-Athlete Commodity

I argue that WMMA subjecthood reflects a shift in the experience of women athletes from the "female-athlete paradox" (Felshin 1974) to the "female-athlete commodity." I propose this term, "female-athlete commodity," to describe how WMMA athletes are flipping the "female-athlete paradox" on its head by *capitalizing* on the perceived "paradox" of their participation in sport rather than trying to reconcile it. Rather than presenting themselves as "strong *but* feminine" athletes (Nelson 1998), then, WMMA athletes are presenting themselves as "strong *and* feminine athletes" (Bruce 2016; McClearen 2021), thereby elevating themselves above other women who merely have the ability to be strong *or* feminine. In this way, WMMA athletes are able to market themselves as "exceptional" women who have the power to "do both," and leverage the appeals of both femininity and masculinity to distinguish themselves in an "economy of visibility" (Banet-Weiser 2015) that privileges hegemonic masculinity and emphasized femininity over queerness, and whiteness over all other races (McClearen 2021).

THE FEMALE-ATHLETE COMMODITY

Doing Both

Contrary to other studies that have found the competing demands of femininity and athleticism to be a source of frustration and anxiety for women athletes (e.g., Adams, Schmitke, and Franklin 2005; Blinde and Taub 1992; Davis-Delano, Pollock, and Vose 2009; Felshin 1974; George 2005; Hardy 2015; Krane et al. 2004; Mennesson 2000), the athletes in this study saw the paradoxical nature of their woman-athlete subjectivities as a source of pride, supporting claims that the image of the sportswoman is becoming more complex and contradictory (Thorpe, Toffoletti, and Bruce 2017). When asked if these athletes had any trouble balancing these dual subjectivities, most of them stated that they did not. In fact, several of the athletes specifically cited the duality of these subjectivities as particularly "fun" or "exciting."

> I like the duality of it. It makes life a little more exciting. (Ruby, 25, Asian, straight).

> It's hot chicks being violent. There's something about it—the clash of the feminine and masculine coming together. The masculine act of fighting but the femininity of beautiful women doing it. (Shannon, 28, white, straight)

This duality was also central to the way in which many athletes in this study chose to market themselves—particularly those who occupied the privileged position of white, heterosexual, and conventionally attractive—as their woman-athlete subjectivities were commodified into brand identities that highlighted the paradoxical nature of these dual subjectivities. These brand identities often consisted of nicknames such as "Lady Killer" or "Pretty Badass," and strategically positioned these women to capitalize on the perceived incongruity of their dual status as combat sports athletes and heterofeminine women. For example, Scarlett (32, white, straight), who markets herself as a "lover *and* a fighter," explained that her former career as a model aided in her ability to draw attention to herself.

> I used to do modeling for a while and so I think that actually helped a lot with my entire career as an amateur because there wasn't a lot of girly girls, then. It was very, very slim. And I think that helped a lot 'cause people were like, "Oh, wow! She's really girly, she does modeling, *and* she can fight."

Similarly, Kani (22, white, straight), who markets herself as a "warrior princess," explained that she sees herself as someone who can switch comfortably between doing masculinity and femininity, marking a shift from the "apologetic" behaviors that have been found in prior studies (Adams, Schmitke, and Franklin 2005; Blinde and Taub 1992; Davis-Delano, Pollock, and Vose 2009; Ezzell 2009; George 2005; Mennesson 2000) and signaling a new female-athlete subject who is both self-aware and indifferent toward the competing demands of sport and society. She explained, "At home, I'm completely different than how I am in a fight. I want to be a good little housewife. But, when it comes down to handling business, I handle *business*."

It is important to distinguish, however, that by "doing both," WMMA athletes are neither "undoing" (Deutsch 2007; Risman 2009) nor "redoing" (West and Zimmerman 2009) gender by challenging its conception as an expression of a binary sex category; instead, they are *reproducing* gender by marketing themselves as *exceptional* women who simply have the power to do "both." This was also evident in the recent social media "empowerment" campaign in which WMMA athletes participated under the hashtag, #GetYouAGirlThatCanDoBoth. The hashtag #GetYouAGirlThatCanDoBoth implicitly refers to the ability to do "both" masculine combat sports violence *and* heterofemininity, and it appeals to a heteropatriarchal gaze by encouraging the athletes' followers to "get" women such as themselves. By "doing both," however, WMMA athletes are able to capitalize on tropes of agentic postfeminist subjecthood to market themselves in ways that allow them to benefit from their association with both hegemonic masculinity and emphasized femininity—both of which are privileged in the "economy of visibility" (Banet-Weiser 2015) that athletes must navigate in order to advance their careers as WMMA athletes (McClearen 2021).

Importantly, such opportunities to market oneself in a way that capitalized on the

perceived incongruity of combat sports talent and heterofemininity were not equally

available to all the athletes who participated in this study—particularly the Black and

queer athletes. For instance, Michelle (32, Black, straight), who was one of fewer than a

handful of Black women in her organization at the time of our interview, explained,

> I think it's a lot easier to see a Black woman as masculine, as opposed to any
> other race. And I think it's because of our darker skin and hair texture and the
> stereotypes we have in America—like being loud and being aggressive. I feel like
> a lot of that plays into the femininity…like the *lack* of femininity. When it comes
> to fans and how I feel I'm marketed and stuff like that, I definitely feel like
> there's a huge difference between me and other women in [my organization].

For Black women such as Michelle, their participation in the masculine sport of MMA is

viewed as less paradoxical and, thus, less exceptional than it is for white women,

decreasing their value as a female-athlete commodity in the eyes of their promoters.

Amanda (29, Black, lesbian) expressed similar sentiments, citing the "politics" of the

sport that limit the exposure of Black women athletes such as herself.

> The women that aren't the "poster girls" but are *talented* aren't getting as much
> exposure and recognition as the ones that maybe their talent is sub-par, but they
> have a pretty face and they're cute and this and that. So, yeah, that hits home
> being in the sport and knowing that there's a lot of politics to it. I know that there
> are certain females in the sport that get more recognition and more attention just
> based on how they look rather than how they perform…where someone like
> myself who has proven my talent kinda' flies under the radar.

Although "doing both" may serve as a new strategy for women athletes to do

gender while competing for attention in economies of visibility (Banet-Weiser 2015), its

reliance on implicitly racialized and (hetero)sexualized performances of femininity

disproportionately harms Black and queer women athletes like Amanda and Michelle

whose performances of femininity are viewed as existing outside of the (white, heterofeminine) "poster girl" image that is most valued in the MMA industry (McClearen 2021). As such, "doing both" serves not as a means to challenge the hegemony of white heterofemininity but rather as a means to maintain privilege for the white heterofeminine athletes who embody it.

Live. Laugh. Love. *Fight.*

WMMA athletes' desires to "do both" are also bolstered by the messages they receive from WMMA media and culture. The promotional campaign for *The Ultimate Fighter Season 20*, "Beauty and Strength," for example, can be interpreted as an advertisement for WMMA athletes' abilities to do both. Through its employment of gendered dichotomies like "jaw-dropping" and "jaw-breaking," and "easy on the eyes" and "hard on the face," the "Beauty and Strength" campaign distinguishes WMMA athletes from other women athletes and non-athletes alike and encourages WMMA fighters to understand their unique value as female-athlete commodities. It also appeals to its (18-34-year-old male) demographic's sense of "both" masculinity and heterosexuality by blending heterosexual men's desires for heterosexy women and masculine combat sports violence.

Popular WMMA apparel companies like Fight Chix, Sicchic, and Fighter Girls also "lean in" to the female-athlete paradox (Felshin 1974) to capitalize on the perceived paradox of fighting femininity. For example, the WMMA "lifestyle brand," Fight Chix, juxtaposes MMA with traditional tropes of white heterofemininity, perhaps best demonstrated by one of its t-shirts that reads, "Live. Laugh. Love. *Fight*." Similarly, in Brazilian jiu-jitsu, companies like Girls in Gis and Fenom Kimonos juxtapose fighting and femininity to appeal to women athletes' postfeminist sensibilities (Gill 2007) and their desire to maintain a feminine identity while participating in masculine sport.

An examination of these companies' websites reveals the influences of neoliberalism and postfeminism in the marketing of their brands, as well as their leveraging of women's empowerment discourse to sell their products. For example, on the Fight Chix website, under "About Us," it reads,

> Since 2006, Fight Chix has become the premiere source for lifestyle and training apparel for women in the mixed martial arts world…Fight Chix has expanded beyond just MMA into fitness, wellness, yoga, crossfit, and jiujitsu…Now, Fight Chix, with its roots in MMA, has a goal to empower all people to reach their full potential and live the Fight Chix lifestyle of being both strong and sexy…We all have challenges in life, but overcoming those challenges is what defines us as a person. Fight Chix wants to be there on your journey to overcome and achieve your potential (FightChix.com).

Fight Chix's mission to "empower all people to reach their full potential and live the Fight Chix lifestyle of being both strong and sexy" is not only strongly reminiscent of the language adopted by the lifestyle brands discussed in Chapter 3, but here strategically employed to market Fight Chix's products to women consumers, specifically, who are presumed to desire to be "both" "strong" and "sexy."

Similarly, the WMMA company, Sicchic, juxtaposes MMA with "traditional" markers of femininity to market themselves as a women-centric MMA brand. For example, an advertisement for its "Cage Cutie" fight skirt reads, "If your [sic] in need of a really cute weigh-in outfit or want to show off your feminine side while throwing elbows – you have come to the right place!" (Sickchic.com). An advertisement for another item, the "Cage Cutie" vale tudo shorts, reads, "Pretty Bad Ass," on the back of the shorts, mirroring the female-athlete nicknames popular among WMMA fighters.

Connecting back to women's empowerment discourse, a t-shirt on its website reads, "All women were created equal. Then, some learn jiu-jitsu," communicating the "exceptional" qualities women fighters are presumed to possess.

The WMMA company, Fighter Girls, employs many of the same tropes discussed above, and features several elements of the female-athlete commodity. Like Fix Chix and Sicchic, their apparel juxtaposes fighting with femininity to cultivate a "bad girl" image, perhaps best demonstrated by their "Fights like a Girl" t-shirt. A description for the t-shirt reads,

> Fights like a Girl/Damn Right I do women's v-neck tee shirt in black. The words speak for themselves. Be proud to fight like a girl, you work hard and your wardrobe should say it! Made of super soft black cotton, this boyfriend cut tee has longer sleeves and body for a more relaxed fit, and a cute v-neck for a feminine touch. The front proclaims, 'Fights Like A Girl' and the back proudly assures the world 'Damn Right I do.' The great mix of flirty script on front and industrial print on back gives this shirt a tough and girly look that you'll love! Be sure to check out this adorably sassy print in our sweat shirt and boyfriend tank too. (FighterGirls.com)

By employing gendered dichotomies like "Fights like a girl" and "Damn right I do," and "tough" and "girly," Fighter Girls is able to market itself as a female-athlete brand, and commodify the "female-athlete paradox" (Felshin 1974) in ways that parallel "doing both." In this way, Fighter Girls distinguishes itself an authentic WMMA brand and allows its consumers to retain their "feminine side" while displaying their "masculine" abilities.

Taken together, the contents of these brands' websites suggest that WMMA athletes are not the only ones attempting to capitalize on the female-athlete paradox (Felshin 1974) by flipping it on its head and "leaning into" the perceived paradox of women fighters. Rather, they suggest that WMMA athletes' gendered performances reflect their subject positions in a gendered "economy of visibility" (Banet-Weiser 2015) that rewards exaggerated performances of "both" masculinity and femininity.

Mom Champs

Themes of motherhood, maternalism, and "true" womanhood are also prominently featured throughout WMMA culture and media. Consider, for example, the way in which WMMA athletes, Montserrat Rendon and Claudia Zamora, were introduced by commentators, Frank Mir and Bryan Lacey, at the previously discussed Freedom Fight Night.

> Lacey: When we look at these two athletes, they're very similar: they're both mothers. Their corners are both their husbands. They have to balance being a mom, being an athlete training to the highest level, as well as balancing that relationship between training with…because they've got active partners who train and compete themselves. Balancing all those dynamics in a household while, what would be classified as selfish, going on this sort of endeavor. It must be a hard thing to juggle.

> Mir: I can't even imagine. I've gotta' be honest with you. 'Cause I'm a father. I have my children. But there's just a different relationship and different responsibility that a woman has with her children and being a mother. I can sit there and go, hey, the woman has the kids—the wife…and I'm gonna' go off and be in the gym. I'm gonna' train and [I] can turn it off. I don't know if women, as mothers, can ever truly shut it down and go straight into training mode. They're always concerned and thinking about their children.

Benevolent sexist tropes about the innate "power" of mothers also serves to maintain patriarchal ideology in WMMA by recasting women's maternity as a noble ideal toward which women should aspire. Perhaps, nowhere is this more evident than in the recent circulation of the term, "mom champ."

The term initially gained popularity after WMMA athlete, Michelle Waterson, declared that she wanted to become the first UFC champion who was also a mother. Shortly thereafter, Waterson's quest to become the first mom champ became a focal point throughout WMMA media, and Waterson herself was even featured in an ESPN documentary, entitled, *Cage Mom* (2019), which centered around her life as a fighter-mother. In the documentary, Waterson—who had previously starred in the 2007 reality television series, *Fight Girls*, and the 2016 documentary film, *Fight Mom*—discusses how her experience as a mother has impacted her career as a fighter, and details the dual subjecthood that she balances as a "fight mom." She explains, "Being a fighter is a completely selfish sport. Being a mother is selfless."

In October of 2019, ESPN released a short documentary-style video of Waterson and fellow "fight mom," Mackenzie Dern, entitled, "Dern, Waterson share goal of being UFC's first mom champ." The video begins with voice-over narration explaining, "They are, perhaps, two of the toughest jobs one can have in the world: fighting professionally inside UFC's Octagon…and being a mom. And believe it or not, there are few women who actually *do both*." The video goes on to explain how in the then-26-year history of the UFC, there had never been a "mom champ," despite several notable fathers earning UFC titles. The video then traces Waterson and Dern's respective journeys through the sport of MMA and shows them discussing how they use their daughters as motivation for their careers. As the video ends, the narrator concludes, "These two women are mothers. And they are fighters. And they are proving these terms are not mutually exclusive."

But neither Waterson nor Dern would become the UFC's first "mom champ." Instead, it was longtime reigning UFC women's bantamweight champion, Amanda Nunes, who was the first to claim this crown. Nunes—an out lesbian who is married to fellow UFC athlete, Nina Nunes—became the UFC's first mom champ on September, 24th, 2020, after her wife gave birth to their first child. An article published to MMA website, MiddleEasy.com, the next day read, "Move over Michelle Waterson, the UFC officially has their first Mom Champ. Featherweight and bantamweight champ Amanda Nunes and her wife Nina Ansaroff have welcomed their newborn daughter into the world" (Hall 2020). This achievement, however, was subsequently contested in ways that demonstrated the politics of motherhood that shape "mom champ" discourse in WMMA.

On December 11th, 2021, at UFC 296, Nunes was defeated by fellow fight mom, Julianna Peña. At the UFC's post-fight press conference, Peña was asked by a reporter, "This is the first time in UFC history that two moms actually fought for a championship. Do you feel the promotion needs to create a new belt for you: The Baddest Mom on the Planet?" Peña responded,

> That is such a great point. The UFC absolutely needs to create a new belt for me. It needs to be, "The Baddest Mom on the Planet." And, you know, I'm not trying to take away anything from Amanda—she's a wonderful mother—but I gave *birth* to my daughter and I know that…you know…I feel like, for giving birth, I am the first mom champ. And that, to me, is also a little feather in the cap.

Peña's statement sparked blowback from fans who interpreted her statements as disrespectful to former champion, Amanda Nunes, as well to other LGBTQ+ and non-birthing mothers who often have their motherhood status challenged in ways that reveal the heteronormative and homophobic assumptions that shape motherhood discourse in heteropatriarchal society (Goldberg, Harbin, and Campbell 2011). Subsequently, in an interview with MMA Junkie, Peña walked back her post-fight comments and claimed that her words had been "misinterpreted." She explained,

> I absolutely had my words misinterpreted. Amanda is an amazing mom. She is an amazing mom champ…Amanda has been such a great champion for the sport and has been a great mom champ as well. But the only thing that I was saying is when I gave birth, I was almost 42 weeks pregnant and I had an emergency C-section where they were like, "We have to get this baby out *now*." I watched them gut me like a fish and take out all of my guts, laid it on the table, and threw it back in and sewed me up. If it wasn't for Mercier Therapy, honestly, I wouldn't be able to get back inside the Octagon. There's so many things that happen to a woman's body when they are pregnant. I was pregnant for 10 months. I had a crazy, very emotional emergency C-section. I didn't know if I was going to fight again. I had to have extra time to bring my body back together to get it back to its peak performance. These are things that happened in my body that I had to do. And to even be able to like feed my baby and nourish my baby from my body. These were incredible moments that only…that mothers, in general, understand, I know, but all I was just saying is, for giving birth…if they're gonna' give Amanda a belt for being mom champ, then I would also like a belt for being mom champ is all I was trying to say.

A few weeks later, Nunes responded via Instagram. In a post addressed to Peña, accompanied by a photo of Nunes with her daughter, she wrote,

> I may not have birthed my Daughter. If I wanted to I could have. I chose to watch from the outside. After going through the IVF procedure with Nina. It was truly heartbreaking to see many women break down in the waiting room knowing they would never be able to carry their own and have to take another direction. This does not make these woman (sic) any less of a MOM than Nina or I. As a MOM champion as well, I feel this needed to be said.

The two eventually met again in a rematch on July 30th, 2022, with Nunes defeating Peña and reclaiming the mom champ moniker.

The UFC, however, is not the only MMA organization to attempt to capitalize on the perceived incongruity of fighting and motherhood. Following the path of the UFC, ONE Championship recently celebrated the arrival of their first mom champ, Angela Lee.

Lee gave birth to her daughter on April 16th, 2021, and returned to the cage less than a year later where she defended her ONE atomweight championship against challenger, Stamp Fairtex. In a video published to the official ONE Championship YouTube page on March 26th, 2022, entitled, "ONE's First-Ever Mom Champ!" Lee is shown just moments after her victory over Fairtex holding her daughter in the ONE Championship cage. Responding to questions from ONE Championship commentator, Mitch Chilson, with her daughter in her arms, Lee stated,

> Guys, this moment right here is a dream come true for me. I wanted to be a world champion and I accomplished that in 2016. Today, March 26th, 2022, I became the first-ever mom champ in ONE Championship. And this little girl right here, she's the reason you guys saw the best performance from me. I trained harder than ever. I pushed myself harder than ever. And because of her, and because of my amazing team, United MMA and United BJJ, I grew and I've transformed into this world champion that you see today. So, thank you, Ava Marie; momma did it for you, baby girl!

Speaking over the applause of the crowd, Chilson then asked, "It looks like you were in a lot of trouble during that first round with that body shot. But we can clearly see that you had a whole other reason to keep going." Lee responded, "You know what? That body shot *hurt*. But I can tell you that my contractions I was having when I was in labor hurt more than that."

CONCLUSION

In this chapter, I have shown how WMMA athletes are flipping the "female-athlete paradox" (Felshin 1974) on its head by "leaning in" to the perceived incongruity of fighting and femininity and marketing themselves as "exceptional" women who have the power to "do both." I have argued that this trend constitutes a shift in the experiences of women athletes from the "female-athlete paradox" to the "female-athlete commodity."

I have also shown how these behaviors are supported by WMMA media and culture, as evidenced by the "fighter girl" lifestyle brands and "mom champ" discourse popular among WMMA athletes. Taken together, these data suggest that WMMA is not an arena in which gender is being "undone" (Deutsch 2007; Risman 2009), but rather, one in which it is being repackaged under neoliberalism.

I stress, however, that WMMA athletes' gender performances are not only motivated by their desires to advance their MMA careers in an "economy of visibility" (Banet-Weiser 2015) that rewards exaggerated performances of "both" hegemonic masculinity and emphasized femininity (McClearen 2021), but also by the increasing desire of neoliberal subjects to be seen as "renaissance" men/women, or individuals with multiple talents and accreditations, in late capitalist society. Skelton and Francis' (2012) work is informative here, as their theorization of "renaissance masculinity" is helpful for understanding the connection between neoliberalism and WMMA athletes' gender performances. As Skelton and Francis (2012: 447) argued about the boys in their study,

> In the same way that the Renaissance Man of the sixteenth century could produce a masculinity which was simultaneously a "complex combination of emotional, sentimental, foppish beau and militaristic aggressor' (Whitehead 2002, 15) the boys discussed here negotiate the masculine/feminine tension in the neoliberal subject.

While Skelton and Francis dismissed the possibility of a "renaissance femininity," the behaviors of the athletes in this study suggest that this may need rethinking. So, too, do the gender performances of numerous women "influencers" in traditionally "masculine" arenas who also seem to cultivate a "renaissance femininity" in order to display their human capital across a number of gendered "economies of visibility" (Banet-Weiser

2015). For example, the popular lifestyle brands, Girls with Guns and Girls Who Lift, include many of the same postfeminist tropes displayed by WMMA brands, Fight Chix, Sicchic, and Fighter Girls, complete with "Back the Blue leggings" and "concealed carry purses" in the case of Girls with Guns (GWGClothing.com), and a "Beauty x Beast/Boss Babe" clothing line in the case of Girls Who Lift (GWLFitness.com). The similarities across these brands suggests that women's desires to "do both" are not unique to the athletes in WMMA but are likely pervasive across a number of neoliberal industries.

By the same token, I would not dismiss the possibility of "doing both" in men's MMA. Indeed, I, myself, have to some degree participated in this as a "fighting scholar" (Garcia and Spencer 2013; Wacquant 2014), and have likewise cultivated what can be interpreted as a "renaissance masculinity" (Skelton and Francis 2012). In fact, my own martial arts students have sometimes jokingly asked about the "Clark Kent" side of my identity—a wholly unearned reference to Superman's citizen alter ego—and expressed amusement over the juxtaposition of my dual careers as an MMA coach and sociologist. In fact, the manager of one of The Mean Girls even asked if I would consider fighting again, upon learning about my experience in both MMA and academia. When I said that I would not, he expressed disappointment, stating, "That's too bad. If [the MMA promotion] found out about your Ph.D., they would *love* you." While the process of "doing both" would likely differ for men—and would likely feature a juxtaposition of two competing masculinities rather than masculinity and femininity—there seems ample reason to believe that such a phenomenon is already occurring. Future research should explore this possibility to better understand the parameters of the "female-athlete

commodity" and neoliberal subjects' increasing desires to "do both."

CHAPTER V: YOU KINDA WANT SOMEONE WHO IS ABLE TO BEAT YOU UP BUT WILL NEVER DO IT: DOING HETEROSEXUALITY IN WMMA

In the documentary, *Through My Father's Eyes: The Ronda Rousey Story* (Stretch, 2019), a memorable moment occurs when director, Gary Stretch, asks the mixed martial arts (MMA) superstar about her dating life. The exchange goes as follows:

> Stretch: So, let me ask you about the boys. I mean, it must be tough when you date a chick who can knock you out, right? I mean, you're really pretty, you're feminine, and you're beautiful. I think you're quite funny. But, when the shit hits the fan, you can knock most of your boyfriends out, so, do men get insecure with you?
>
> Rousey: Well, I think some *would*, but I think that just kinda helps me with the filter process. If anyone's insecure with being with someone like me, they never ask me [out] and I don't have to deal with insecure guys.

The documentary then quickly cuts to a conversation between Stretch and Rousey's judo trainer, the late "Judo" Gene LeBell.

> LeBell: She's gonna live to be the world's oldest virgin—her mother loves this story—because she'll go out with any guy that could *beat* her.

The documentary then abruptly cuts to a montage of Rousey throwing men to the ground with her signature judo techniques before cutting back to LeBell.

> LeBell: A lot of guys have tried. She's still a virgin.

While the topic allows for a humorous exchange between Stretch and LeBell, it also provokes an interesting sociological question: how do women combat sports athletes "do" heterosexuality (West and Zimmerman 1987; Schilt and Westbrook 2009) in their intimate relationships, given the gender-transgressive nature of their status as women fighters? Such is the focus of this chapter.

While women's participation in other "masculine" sports has been discussed as "transgressive" and "empowering," it has been argued that women's participation in MMA holds the power to be particularly subversive, as it "challenge[s] a traditional and fundamental pillar of male dominance" (Mierzwinski, Velija, and Malcolm 2014: 74). Jakubowska et al. (2016: 425), for example, argued that WMMA athletes held potential to "challenge, subvert, and re-write traditional gendered logic," by challenging the perception of women as physically weak, and troubling the discursive relationship between fighting and masculinity. Alsarve and Tjønndal (2020: 485) argued, similarly, that WMMA athletes held potential to act as "female role models" through their "counter-hegemonic negotiation of norms and views of 'traditional' femininity and, more specifically, the perception of femininity as something fragile and passive." Channon and Matthews (2015: 6) highlighted this gender-subversive potential as well, arguing that women fighters not only challenged enduring myths of "natural" female frailty and passivity but also "depart[ed] from the normative construction of women as vulnerable to and dependent upon men for protection."

No study to date, however, has examined the heterosexual relationships of WMMA athletes. Because WMMA athletes are understood to be "empowered," one might expect them to enjoy greater power in their intimate relationships than their non-fighting peers. Mennesson's (2000) study of women's boxing provides support for this rationale, as she reported that the women boxers in her study presented themselves as "liberated" women and claimed to have more egalitarian relationships with their male partners. Whether this is occurring in WMMA, however, remains an unanswered question.

In this chapter, I draw once again from my interviews with professional WMMA athletes ($N = 40$) to examine how WMMA athletes "do" heterosexuality (West and Zimmerman 1987; Schilt and Westbrook 2009) in their intimate relationships. I begin by outlining my theoretical framework before presenting my findings. I find that the heterosexual WMMA athletes in my study accomplish heterofemininity in their intimate relationships through three specific actions: (1) partnering with men who are physically larger than them, (2) partnering with men who are physically stronger and/or more powerful than them, and (3) adhering to heteropatriarchal scripts. I argue therefore that women's participation in MMA does not lead to greater power in their intimate relationships. Finally, I conclude with a discussion of how heterosexual norms may contribute to instances of intimate partner violence (IPV) within the mixed martial arts community.

DOING GENDER AND SEXUALITY IN WOMEN'S SPORTS

Doing Gender, Doing Heterosexuality

Gender is a social structure that is embedded in the individual, interactional, and institutional dimensions of our society (Risman 2018). At the interactional level, it is maintained through a highly routinized system of performing "manhood" and "womanhood," or what West and Zimmerman (1987) termed, "doing" gender. West and Zimmerman's "doing gender" framework illuminates how even the most routine actions are often shaped in accordance with one's gender identity, or what it means to be "masculine" or "feminine" by a particular society. Through this lens, gender is not something we "are" but rather something we "do."

In heteronormative societies, where heterosexuality is considered to be the most "normal" and "natural" form of sexuality, gendered expectations are constructed around the presumption of heterosexual relations between women and men (Butler 1990; Schilt and Westbrook 2009; West and Zimmerman, 1987). To do gender "normally," then, is to also "do" heterosexuality (Butler 1990; Schilt and Westbrook 2009; West and Zimmerman 1987). This "heterosexual matrix" (Butler 1990) upholds the sex/gender binary and hierarchy of male/masculine over female/feminine and imposes normative roles and behaviors that maintain a system of heteropatriarchy (Song et al. 2023; Ward 2020). Importantly, normative constructions of gender and sexuality are also shaped by race and reveal a legacy of white supremacy and settler colonialism (Arvin, Tuck, and Morrill 2013; Vidal-Ortiz, Robinson, and Khan 2018; Ward 2020). Doing normative heterosexuality, therefore, requires investment in the maintenance of gender inequality and whiteness.

West and Zimmerman (1987) show how heterosexual norms play a key role in the maintenance of gender difference and inequality through their discussion of assortative partnering. They explain,

> Assortative mating practices among heterosexual couples afford still further means to create and maintain differences between women and men. For example, even though size, strength, and age tend to be normally distributed among females and males (with considerable overlap between them), selective pairing ensures couples in which boys and men are visibly bigger, stronger, and older (if not "wiser") than the girls and women with whom they are paired. So, should situations emerge in which greater size, strength, or experience is called for, boys

and men will be ever ready to display it and girls and women, to appreciate its display (West and Zimmerman 1987: 138).

As West and Zimmerman (1987) illuminate, by selectively partnering with intimate partners whose traits display contrast with their own gender identity, heterosexuals not only reinforce their own gender identities but also reproduce the social construction of the gender binary and hierarchy. Indeed, hypergamy—the practice of forming a relationship with a person of higher sociological status—is a historical feature of heterosexual relations in patriarchal societies (Ward 2020). This is, perhaps, best captured in the phrase "marrying up," wherein women in heteropatriarchal societies are encouraged to partner with men of higher sociological status, as women's access to power in these societies has historically been through men. Modern heterosexual norms reveal the endurance of this hypergamy, as contemporary studies show how heterosexual women continue to partner with men who are taller (Tao 2020), older (Moore et al. 2006), and higher income earners (Qian 2017) than themselves.

Doing Heterosexuality in Women's Sports

Feminist sport scholars have long documented the pressures women athletes face to conform to heterosexual norms and ideals (Blinde and Taub 1992; Felshin 1974; Kolnes 1995; Krane 2001; Krane et al. 2004; Lock 2003; Mean and Kassing 2008; Messner 1996; Mohapatra 2021; Wright and Clark 1999). Messner (1996) for example, argued that, while sport participation served to confirm men's masculinity and heterosexuality (i.e., athleticism = masculinity = heterosexuality), for women athletes, their participation in sport more often served to call their femininity and heterosexuality into question (i.e., athleticism? femininity? heterosexuality?), leading some women athletes to emphasize their femininity and heterosexuality out of fear or stigmatization.

Blinde and Taub (1992) argued, similarly, that women athletes were confronted by a

"lesbian stigma," due to their transgressing "traditional" boundaries of heterosexual

femininity, leading many of these athletes to adopt various techniques to control and

manage information about their sexual identities. Knight and Giuliano (2003) showed

how sports media contributed to the "compulsory heterosexuality" (Rich 1980) that

shapes women athletes' experiences by emphasizing their participation in stereotypically

feminine activities and displaying their relationships with their heterosexual male

partners.

Very few studies, however, have examined the intimate relationships of women

athletes. The few studies that have investigated these relationships have largely portrayed

them as conforming to heteropatriarchal norms and expectations. Krane et al. (2004), for

example, found that the women athletes in their study made efforts to conform to

heterofeminine ideals to attract heterosexual male partners. Bennett et al. (2017) found

that the women athletes in their study made efforts to partner with men who were

physically larger than them to "emphasize" their heterofemininity in their intimate

relationships. Researchers have also found that female athlete-male coach intimate

relationships are not uncommon in women's sports, and often lead to abuses of power

that are shaped by heteropatriarchal ideals (Brake 2011; Bringer, Brackenridge, and

Johnston 2002; Gaedicke et al. 2021; Johannson and Larsson 2011; Tomlinson and

Yorganci 1997). Whether and how these dynamics manifest in the context of WMMA

athletes' intimate relationships, however, remains an unanswered question.

Doing Heterosexuality in Women's Combat Sports

While the women's sports literature demonstrates how women athletes' intimate relationships often conform to heterosexual norms, women combat sports athletes may be an exception to this trend, as women fighters transgress boundaries of "traditional" heterosexual femininity by demonstrating women's capacity for physical violence and domination (Channon and Matthews 2015; Mierzwinski, Velija, and Malcolm 2014). Mennesson's (2000) study of women's boxing offers hope for this thesis, as she showed how the women boxers in her study rejected the "homemaker" role that was modeled by their mothers and challenged patriarchal gender relations in their households. As Mennesson (2000: 30) explained,

> These women were able to challenge conventional sex roles in the household, even though the models provided by their mothers did not predispose them to question their status. In building this "liberated" identity, the process of secondary socialization and biography interact. For instance, the women's coaches held relatively progressive attitudes concerning gender roles (e.g. supporting the women's pursuit of a university education) and were critical of professionalism in their sport. These boxers' social mobility complemented their leisurely relationship to the sport and was consonant with the identity of the "emancipated woman" that they articulated.

As this study suggests, women fighters may be more resistant to heterosexual norms than other women athletes, as their gender transgressions in sport may extend into their intimate relationships.

Yet there is also evidence to suggest that this is not occurring in WMMA. While scholarly research in this area is currently scant, depictions of fighter relationships in MMA media suggest that these relationships are frequently troubled and, often, even violent. Indeed, numerous MMA athletes have been arrested and incarcerated for various forms of intimate partner violence (IPV) (see Bohn 2017; Debets 2018; Lewis 2019; Marrocco 2019; Martin 2021; Meshew 2018; Okamoto 2018; Ordoñez 2021; Wells and Samano 2021; Raimondi 2016; Raimondi 2018; Raimondi 2021) and, increasingly, women MMA athletes are being revealed to be the victims of these assaults (Lewis 2019; Meshew 2018; Okamoto 2018; Ordoñez 2021; Raimondi 2018). In 2018, for example, it was revealed that UFC star, Andrea Lee, had been assaulted by her husband, Donny Aaron, who allegedly extinguished a lit cigarette on her arm before beginning to strangle her (Raimondi 2018). Just a few months later, fellow UFC fighter, Rachael Ostovich, was hospitalized with a broken orbital bone, following an alleged attack by her husband, Arnold Berdon, who she accused of repeatedly punching her in the face and body (Okamoto 2018). In 2021, former UFC champion, Nicco Montaño, alleged that she had been assaulted by fellow fighter, Justin Watson, who she accused of standing on her neck and "stomping" on her face before she was able to flee their hotel room (Ordoñez 2021). In 2023, TMZ even obtained a video of UFC President, Dana White, assaulting his wife in public while celebrating New Year's Eve at a Cabo San Lucas nightclub (TMZ 2023), While these are just a few anecdotal accounts, they nevertheless provide reason for skepticism regarding the extension of any gender-subversive potential into the realm of WMMA athletes' intimate relationships, as these accounts depict fighter relationships as sites of patriarchal violence and control.

DOING HETEROSEXUALITY IN WMMA

In this section, I draw from my interviews with WMMA athletes to examine how these athletes "do" heterosexuality (West and Zimmerman 1987; Schilt and Westbrook

2009) in their intimate relationships. I find that, unlike the women boxers in Mennesson's (2000) study, WMMA athletes conform to "traditional" heteropatriarchal norms in their heterosexual relationships, as evidenced both by their intimate partner choices and relationship experiences. I find that WMMA athletes accomplish heterofemininity in these relationships through three actions in particular: (1) partnering with men who are physically larger than them, (2) partnering with men who are physically stronger and/or more powerful than them, and (3) adhering to heteropatriarchal scripts. I argue, therefore, that women's participation in MMA does not lead to greater power in their intimate relationships.

Maintaining Sexual Dimorphism

Among the most taken-for-granted assumptions about men and women in Western society is that men are *supposed* to be bigger and stronger than women. So, while average size and strength differences between women and men are rooted in biology, they are also perpetuated by our intimate partner choices. Because heterosexual norms prescribe heteropatriarchal roles of protector and provider to male partners and nurturer and caregiver to female partners, the institution of heterosexuality has a vested interest in maintaining sexual dimorphism between women and men, "so, should situations emerge in which greater size, strength, or experience is called for, boys and men will be ever ready to display it and girls and women, to appreciate its display (West and Zimmerman 1987: 138). This white, Christian construction of the "normal" heterosexual couple shapes men and women's sexual and romantic desires and serves the maintenance of heteropatriarchy and white supremacy. This uniquely impacts women athletes who are often physically larger and/or more muscular than many (if not most) of the non-athlete men they encounter in their daily lives (Bennett et al. 2017).

Consistent with heteropatriarchal norms, the athletes in this study exhibited a strong preference for male partners who were physically taller, heavier, and more muscular than themselves. In fact, out of the 31 athletes in the study who identified as heterosexual, just 2 of them said that they did not have a preference for dating taller men. Just 5 of the 31 athletes who identified as heterosexual said that they did not have a preference for dating heavier men. These relative size preferences were far less pronounced for the athletes who did not identify as heterosexual, with just 2/9 of these athletes stating a relative height or weight preference for their romantic partners.

When I asked the heterosexual athletes why they exhibited such a strong preference for partnering with bigger men, they revealed that it was because partnering with bigger men made them feel smaller and, thus, more feminine. By partnering with men who were physically larger than themselves, even the athletes in my study who were taller or heavier than their peers could feel small and feminine in the presence of their intimate partners and, thus, accomplish heterofemininity in their intimate relationships. As one athlete in my study explained, "When I'm with a guy who's smaller, it makes me feel bigger. And, I don't wanna' feel bigger because bigger means fatter or undesirable or unpretty" (Kristina, 30, mixed race). Similarly, another athlete explained, "I don't think I can date somebody smaller than me. 'Cause I wouldn't feel feminine" (Grace, 36, Asian). Indeed, several of the athletes specifically cited concerns about femininity as the reason for their insistence on partnering with larger men.

> I like being shorter because it's more comfortable…Because what I do is so masculine, a lot of the times things that make me feel feminine, like feeling small, as a female, I really like those things to kind of bring balance to myself…It's really nice to be able to look pretty and feel dainty and feminine and small. (Shannon, 28, white)

> Yeah. I do [like being shorter than my partners]…It goes back to the whole, like, I don't wanna' feel *bigger*. And then I guess maybe it's a little masculine in relationship terms. (Alice, 27, white)

> I dated a guy that I was taller than and…you wear heels and it's like you feel more masculine. (Scarlett, 32, white)

Partnering with men who were taller, heavier, and more muscular than themselves was, therefore, one strategy through which WMMA athletes accomplished heterofemininity in their intimate relationships.

"Real" Men and "Real" Women

In discussing their preference for masculine partners, the athletes in my study revealed that this preference was not only motivated by their desire to feel feminine, but also by their desire to feel like "real" women. It was, therefore, of paramount importance to these women that they partnered with *real* men. To these women, there was no clearer marker of "real" manhood than a man's ability to fight. Perhaps, unsurprisingly, then, the heterosexual athletes in my study exhibited a strong preference for dating fellow fighters. Indeed, out of the 31 heterosexual athletes I interviewed, 26 of them were currently or had formerly been in relationships with other fighters or coaches. As they athletes explained,

> My husband is lucky he could beat my ass…If I could beat your ass, I'm always gonna' look at you like a little brother. I'm never gonna' look at you like this guy that I could potentially date…It's kinda weird, it's like you kinda want someone who is able to beat you up but will never do it. (Michelle, 32, Black)

It goes back to the whole, like, feeling protected and having a guy that's more masculine than you are…When I'm in the gym, I might come out looking like a cavewoman. So, you know, having a guy who's more of a caveman than I am is nice…And, for female fighters, that's a hard thing to find outside of the gym…of course you have guys that are big gnarly dudes, but…in general, if I pick a random guy off the street and he's never fought a day in his life, then I'll probably feel like I might be a little more masculine than him. And as I said, that's not something I would want in a relationship. (Jasmine, 27, Asian)

I like to be able to give my partner a good run for their money, physically, but I don't really like to win. I don't. Because, I just…biologically…I think I'm just attracted to masculine men. They have to be more masculine than me because I am a woman and there is supposed to be a difference. (Megan, 31, white)

When asked whether they would be willing to partner with men who were not as physically powerful as them, many of the athletes echoed this sentiment, explaining that it would be difficult to see such men as "real" men.

I don't know if I could [date a man who wasn't as physically powerful as me]. I feel like if I can beat you up, then there's a little bit of problem with that…If I'm with a man, I wanna' be with a *man*. (Kani, 22, white)

I feel like, as a *man*…my boyfriend should be able to defend me. Like, if we were in a situation, he should definitely be stronger than me. (Chloe, 23, Hispanic/Latina)

So, I obviously have a slightly masculine side to me. I think any woman that is into fighting does. But at the same time, I have the part of me that's very girly and very traditional…I want a big, strong, sexy man that can *throw* me. I don't think I'd be attracted to someone not in that category. (Jasmine, 27, Asian)

The athletes' desire to feel like "real" women ultimately revealed a desire for normalcy, reflecting Ward's (2015: 35) claim that heterosexuality is, in part, a "fetishization of the normal." Being stronger and/or more powerful than their male partners, as the athletes made clear, was anything but "normal," and was, therefore, antagonistic to the accomplishment of heterosexuality.

When I tried to date guys that weren't fighters…they didn't get it. Like, they were kind of beta to me 'cause they just thought it was so cool that I was a girl that fought…I kind of need another alpha next to me. Like, I don't want somebody that's just like, "Oh, it's so cool that my girlfriend could kick my ass!"…That's just not…it doesn't work. (Kelly, 39, white)

Well, I think looks-wise, too, I think everyone with social media—especially this generation—everyone just wants that cute social media couple post…And I'm super stocky. I have a total wrestler body…And so looking at me next to like a skinny guy would look kinda awkward, I guess. (Chloe, 23, Hispanic/Latina)

For some athletes, even partnering with male fighters of lesser skill or experience would be antagonistic to their accomplishment of "normalcy," and would therefore be unappealing.

Like, honestly, I will not date a lower belt or like even hook up with them. I mean, there are some attractive guys that I've seen and I'm like, "Oh, he's beautiful." And then I find out that he's a lower belt and I'm like, ah, never mind. The attraction level just like plummeted. (Leilani, 28, Hawaiian)

It's kinda weird if they don't have a black belt. 'Cause now it's like I'm dating a lower belt which is just like an awkward thing. (Madelyn, 29, white)

By partnering with bigger, stronger, more experienced male fighters, however, these athletes could fulfill their desire for normalcy and accomplish "real" womanhood.

Tradwives

In addition to partnering with bigger, stronger, more powerful men, the athletes in my study also demonstrated a strong adherence to "traditional" heteropatriarchal scripts, such as through their desire to become "housewives" and have their partners serve as the "leaders" and "protectors" of their households. Indeed, the athletes' descriptions of their ideal male partners were largely consistent with what Young (2003) refers to as the "masculine protectionist," which describes the "traditional" heteropatriarchal male figure who is willing to risk his own safety to ensure the protection of his family. According to

Young (2003), central to the logic of the masculine protectionist is the subordinate

relation of those being protected. As Young (2003: 4-5) explains,

> In return for male protection, the woman concedes critical distance from decision-making autonomy. When the household lives under a threat, there cannot be divided wills and arguments about who will do what, or what is the best course of action. The head of the household should decide what measures are necessary for the security of the people and property, and he gives the orders that they must follow if they and their relations are to remain safe…Feminine subordination, in this logic, does not constitute submission to a violent and overbearing bully. The feminine woman, rather, on this construction, adores her protector and happily defers to his judgment in return for the promise of security that he offers.

Consistent with this notion, the athletes expressed desires to allow their male partners to

"lead" while they remained subordinate in order to bring "balance" to their relationships.

As they explained,

> I feel like...happier homes have men left to be the lead in some way—made to think that they're important or an authority…I feel like that's very natural. Not that women shouldn't be supported or have important roles or things like that but...there has to be that balance, I guess. (Gabriella, 30, white)

> A man is supposed to provide security—and that means financially, physically, emotionally…I think that it's his job to create a stable home. Period. And, I think, for a woman, it's her job to tend it, to care for it, to provide the love. To provide that feminine, that softness, to that security…I think a woman's role is to provide the love and the gentle side. (Page, 31, Hispanic/Latina)

> My dad provided for the family and my mom was the housewife. That's like the ideal lifestyle for me. Like, I'm all about women working a lot and stuff like that but I feel like the woman is the backbone of the home and if you run a good household, your kids will come out right…There are some that want the woman to be the boss and it's so weird to me…I don't understand how a man could sit in the home while his woman is working. It's like what is wrong with this picture? *You* shouldn't be cooking. (Maria, 29, Hispanic/Latina)

While some of the athletes acknowledged these arrangements as "old school" or even

"sexist," they nevertheless characterized these arrangements as "normal" and "natural" to

justify their adherence to these heteropatriarchal conventions.

Well, like I said, I'm old school. Like, I think the guy should be a certain way. Handle certain things. Be the leader, I guess. More of the alpha or whatever you wanna call it. And the woman should take a little bit of a back seat…Just the basic dynamic of how it should be. (Madelyn, 29, white)

It's still kind of like old school and I guess it is a little sexist but that's just how I was raised. Like my dad would always pay for my mom when they went out to dinner. Like, he wants to take her out to dinner. He should pay for it. You know what I mean? It's kind of sexist but it's just kind of how I was raised and kind of believe, I guess. (Autumn, 29, white)

While these "traditional" heteropatriarchal arrangements stood in stark contrast to the gender-transgressive behaviors the athletes displayed in their professional sporting careers, the athletes nevertheless characterized these arrangements as indicative of "normal" heterofeminine behavior. As one athlete explained, "At home I'm completely different than how I am in a fight. I want to be a good little housewife. But when it comes down to handling business, I handle *business*" (Kani, 22, white).

The athletes' "traditional" patriarchal arrangements paralleled the "tradwife" lifestyle that has received renewed support in recent years, thanks in part to its promotion by conservative and far-right activists in online spaces (Lavin 2020; Mattheis 2018). According to Mattheis (2018), the "tradwife"—a compound, Internet-based term meaning "traditional wife"—represents a "traditional," conservative (white) woman who sees herself as overcoming the "false consciousness" of leftist movements, such as feminism, multiculturalism, and anti-racism, through a return to "traditional" (white) heteropatriarchal ideals. She argues that the "tradwife" movement is a response to women's increased anxieties about marriage, femininity, and family in late capitalism, and has itself become a useful tool in recruiting women—especially white women—into far-right and white supremacist movements. Mattheis (2018: 155) also illuminates the relationship between the "tradwife" and postfeminism, through her analysis of alt-right

blogger, Lana Lokteff. She explains,

> Using McRobbie's notion of post-feminism as a contemporary sensibility, we can
> see that Lokteff also stokes white women's fears about marriage and family.
> These fears include anxieties over finding a husband, aging out of having children
> for unmarried women, and aging out for women who do not have children but
> desire to become mothers. And, for women who are already married or divorced,
> these discourses invoke fear of loss of husbands or a framing for why a marriage
> failed. For example, Ayla Stewart, a Lokteff acolyte and tradwife blogger of "A
> Wife with Purpose," believes her marriage failed because she did not honor the
> "natural" gendered roles Lokteff asserts (Darby 4). Moreover, for women with
> children, especially mothers of sons, these narratives stoke their fears about their
> sons' unfair treatment, such as false rape accusations in a society that wrongly
> favors women because of feminism run amok. This, in particular, links to other
> current discursive frameworks from opposition to the #MeToo movement to the
> rhetoric of online misogynist groups, including Men's Rights Activists (MRAs),
> Men Going Their Own Way (MGTOW), and Pick Up Artists (PUA). It is these
> fears derived from a postfeminist sensibility that ease the way for mainstreaming
> and making sensible the more explicitly racist, xenophobic, antisemitic, and hate-
> based ideology.

For the WMMA athletes in this study, their "traditional" relationship lifestyles

included performing domestic tasks like cooking and cleaning, as well as performing

"submissiveness" to their male partners. As several of the athletes explained,

> I'm okay with being in a submissive position to the male counterpart…I wouldn't
> mind them taking a little bit of the lead, you know? I'm fine with that. I don't have
> a problem with that. As long as it's not abuse…it's not a negative role. Just
> because you wanna' be submissive to your significant other, your husband, or
> anything like that; I don't think there's anything wrong with that…I trust you to
> lead. That's all that submissiveness means to me: I trust you to lead…I think that's
> a really good way to put it. (Alice, 27, white)

> My role as a wife has changed…you could have interviewed me four years ago
> and I would have had the exact opposite answers to all these questions. However,
> I've done a lot of reading and reading marriage books and, like, relationship
> roles…And so, that more submissive [role]…I see the results that I get for being
> more feminine to him and I do, I like that. I didn't understand that I wanted that
> but now that I've read and learned more, I definitely do. (Page, 31,
> Hispanic/Latina)

I would say, yeah, I do [like to be the submissive partner in my relationships]. I guess I'm kind of old fashioned in that sense. I like a man to be the man. I like the man to take the lead. Not that I'm the kind of person that will never do my own thing or never voice my own opinion or say, "I wanna do this," but I also like a man that is a *man*. And he's not afraid to stand on his own two feet. Or say, "I don't agree with you. This is the final thing." Okay, then we'll do that. I grew up in a very religious household, so I carry some of those standards still. (Nicole, 53, white)

While these arrangements exemplified the patriarchal structure of "normal" heterosexuality, they nevertheless allowed the athletes to accomplish "traditional" heterofemininity in their intimate relationships and alleviate any potential concerns around femininity brought on by their hypermasculine careers. Adhering to heteropatriarchal scripts was, therefore, a common strategy through which the athletes accomplished heterosexuality in their intimate relationships.

CONCLUSION

In this chapter, I have shown how WMMA athletes "do" heterosexuality (West and Zimmerman 1987; Schilt and Westbrook 2009) in their intimate relationships by conforming to "traditional" heteropatriarchal ideals. More specifically, I have shown how WMMA athletes accomplish heterofemininity in these relationships through three distinct actions: (1) partnering with men who are physically larger than them, (2) partnering with men who are physically stronger and/or more powerful than them, and (3) adhering to heteropatriarchal scripts. I conclude, therefore, that women's participation in WMMA does not lead to their holding greater power in their intimate relationships or experiencing greater equality in their relationships than their non-fighting peers.

While WMMA athletes' conformity to heteropatriarchal ideals are not exceptional—particularly when you consider the pervasiveness of conservative and postfeminist ideology in modern sport (Garcia and Proffitt 2022; Nash 2018; Toffoletti, Francombe-Webb, and Thorpe 2018)—they are nevertheless concerning given the growing epidemic of intimate partner violence (IPV) in the mixed martial arts community and the recent trend of WMMA athletes being revealed to be the victims of relationship violence and abuse. By limiting themselves to partnering with bigger, stronger male fighters and adhering to heteropatriarchal scripts in their intimate relationships, women MMA athletes may indeed be increasing their likelihood of experiencing IPV. Many of the athletes I interviewed had in fact experienced some form of IPV in their current or previous relationships—or personally knew of a fellow WMMA athlete who had—and almost all of these instances included male fighters or coaches. WMMA athletes would do well to distance themselves from these relationships and cultivate healthier romantic bonds.

Finally, studying the intimate relationships of WMMA athletes reveals the ways in which men's domination of women is not only normalized in heteropatriarchal society but also transformed into a "normal" sexual and romantic desire. Statements such as, "I like to be able to give my partner a good run for their money, physically, but I don't really like to win," and, "You kinda want someone who is able to beat you up but will never do it," exemplify this phenomenon and demonstrate the linkages between heterosexuality, patriarchy, and violence against women. While the athletes in this study transgressed boundaries of "traditional" heterosexual femininity in their sporting careers, contributing to the popular perception of them as "empowered" women athletes, these

athletes' desires for "normal" heterosexual relationships ultimately undermined these

transgressions and limited the potentially "empowering" effects of their participation in

MMA. Feminist sport scholars should, therefore, continue to examine the ways in which

the institution of heterosexuality undermines the effects of women's participation in sport

and serves as a barrier women's empowerment and liberation. Future research should

also call greater attention to the false appeals of the "tradwife" lifestyle and continue to

illuminate its connections to neoliberalism, postfeminism, and far-right and white

supremacist ideology.

CHAPTER VI: BEYOND BREAKING BARRIERS: RETHINKING WOMEN'S EMPOWERMENT IN SPORT

In this dissertation, I have attempted to provide the most thorough sociological account of women's mixed martial arts (WMMA) to date. Drawing from multiple qualitative research methods, including ethnography, content analysis, and semi-structured interviews ($N = 40$), I have tried to construct a more complete picture of WMMA athletes' social worlds than that which has been provided by prior studies and offer a theoretically-informed assessment of WMMA's potential as a site for the empowerment of women. In this chapter, I return to the question I posed at the beginning of this project—Are WMMA athletes *really* breaking barriers?—and offer suggestions for how we can move beyond neoliberal-postfeminist conceptions of empowerment through a recommitment to addressing the structures of capitalism, heteropatriarchy, and white supremacy that constrain women's lives.

ARE WMMA ATHLETES REALLY BREAKING BARRIERS?

Empowerment

The primary research question behind this dissertation was whether women's participation in MMA was serving as a form of empowerment. In Chapter 1, I showed how this question was motivated by the framing of WMMA as a space of women's empowerment by both scholars and media, and how this framing stood in contrast to other accounts that suggested that MMA was a regressive space characterized by hypermasculinity, heteropatriarchy, and white supremacy. I also showed how scholars' conceptions of empowerment had changed drastically over time, shifting from feminist calls for structural empowerment to an individualized and apolitical call to harness women's untapped human capital in a world which was presumed to no longer need feminist intervention (Batliwala 2007; Cornwall 2016; Radhakrishnan and Solari 2022). Through this process, I argued, many feminist insights regarding women's empowerment had been lost, but by becoming aware of the history of women's empowerment, we could recover varied collectivist interpretations of empowerment that could help us imagine more equitable paths forward (Radhakrishnan and Solari 2022).

In Chapter 3, I presented data from my interviews with WMMA athletes that directly addressed the question of empowerment. I revealed that while most of the athletes in my sample did consider themselves empowered, these athletes constructed their empowered status primarily in relation to other women, demonstrating the influences of neoliberalism and postfeminism on these athletes' conceptions of empowerment. These athletes, in turn, used these self-conceptions to distance themselves from what they considered "regular women," and, in effect, reproduced patriarchal stereotypes about women's inferiority. This, I argue, is inconsistent with feminist theorizing about empowerment and misrepresents the nature of women's oppression. Rather than a process through which women organize and act against patriarchy, the athletes in this study appeared to understand empowerment as an intra-gender contest wherein women compete against one another in the pursuit of material and symbolic capital. This, in effect, not only limited the individual benefits these women stood to gain from their experience in MMA but also limited the wider epistemological challenge to patriarchy that women as a group might otherwise enjoy through women's collective participation in fighting sports.

In Chapter 5, I showed how WMMA athletes' desires to "do" heterofemininity

(West and Zimmerman 1987; Schilt and Westbrook 2009) in their intimate relationships

further limited the empowerment potential of their participation in MMA. I revealed how

these athletes' desires for "traditional" heterosexual relationships led to their partnering

almost exclusively with fellow combat sports athletes in order to ensure a patriarchal

power dynamic with their male partners maintaining greater physical and social power. I

argued that these athletes accomplished heterofemininity in their intimate relationships

through three actions in particular: (1) partnering with men who were physically larger

than them, (2) partnering with men who were physically stronger and/or more powerful

than them, and (3) adhering to heteropatriarchal scripts. These relationship outcomes, I

argue, are inconsistent with the notion of empowerment and cast further doubt on the

empowerment potential of WMMA.

Physical Feminism

A closely related question to the question of empowerment was whether women's

participation in MMA was serving as a form of "physical feminism" (McCaughey 1997).

In Chapter 1, I described how several scholars had applied McCaughey's (1997) physical

feminism theory to studies of martial arts and combat sports (MACS), and how these

scholars had expressed optimism regarding MACS's potential as a site of physical

feminism (Channon and Phipps 2017; Maor 2019; Noel 2009). I also cited Burke's

(2019) study which argued that McCaughey's (1997) theory was largely being

misappropriated. I ultimately echoed Burke's (2019) contention that several commitments should be made within women's sports to achieve feminist

epistemological-political gains and meet the criteria for physical feminism:

1. The importance of consciousness-raising

2. The need for collective and women-centered organizations

3. A radical challenge to the broader patriarchal discourse, including its

    contextualization in neoliberal capitalism.

In Chapter 3, I presented data from my interviews with WMMA athletes that

revealed the athletes' feelings about male and female biology and the athletes' abilities to

defend themselves against male violence. While for McCaughey (1997), martial arts

training represented an enlightening experience through which women could become

aware of the socially constructed nature of male privilege and gain a critical

consciousnesses of gender's influence on male and female bodies, the athletes in this

study did not appear to have this experience. In fact, paradoxically, it appeared that the

athletes' experiences training with men only seemed to strengthen their beliefs in male

superiority and allow them to justify gender inequality. As explained by one of the

athletes,

> I know I'm a badass, but in the female division. I'm sorry but if a man ran up on
> me, I'm going to do my 100 percent best to try to defend myself. . . but, there's
> just a different strength between a man and a woman. . .there's girls in my fights
> that can take my punches in the first minute and not go down; what do you think a
> man's gonna do? I know I cannot beat up a man. (Kani, 22, white, straight)

Also, in Chapter 3, I presented data from interviews that directly addressed

WMMA athletes' feelings about feminism. Despite scholars' suggestions that WMMA

could become the new "feminist frontier" (Quinney 2016: 55), the vast majority of the athletes in this study were explicitly anti-feminist. Understanding feminism as a restrictive, coercive practice that was both undesirable and unnecessary in their daily lives, these athletes voiced strong disdain for feminists and "the feminist agenda," often even before being asked any questions about feminism. These outcomes, I argue, are inconsistent with the notion of physical feminism (McCaughey 1997) and cast further doubt on the potential of physical feminism in WMMA.

Undoing Gender

Another closely related question to the question of empowerment was whether women's participation in MMA was serving as a form of "undoing gender" (Deutsch 2007; Risman 2009). Because women's empowerment had been theorized not only as a process through which women gain access to, and control of, both material and informational resources (Batliwala 1994), but also a process through which women "redefine gender roles in ways which extend their possibilities for being and doing" (Mosedale 2005: 252), WMMA athletes' "doing" of gender (West and Zimmerman 1987) was of particular interest to this study. In Chapter 1, I explained how several scholars had theorized that MACS represented a space where women could "undo" gender by "appropriat[ing] male symbols of physical capital and shift[ing] gender relations of power" (Davies and Deckert 2018: 15). I also explained how studies by Weaving (2014), Jennings (2015), and McClearen (2015) suggested that WMMA was a space where gender was heavily policed, and even sanctioned. Understanding whether WMMA athletes were "undoing gender" (Deutsch 2007; Risman 2009) by challenging the essentialism of gender as a fixed property of the sexed body was, therefore, an important objective for this study.

In Chapter 4, I discussed the doing and selling of gender in WMMA. I introduced two original concepts, "the female-athlete commodity" and "doing both," to explain the role of gender in WMMA. Using my concept of the female-athlete commodity, I explained how WMMA athletes were flipping the "female-athlete paradox" (Felshin 1974) on its head by "leaning in" to the perceived paradox of fighting and femininity to market themselves as "exceptional" women who had the power to do "both" (masculinity and femininity). Rather than citing this as an example of WMMA athletes "undoing gender," however, I showed how WMMA athletes' doing of "both" revealed both a regressive understanding of gender and a motivation to use their privilege as predominantly white, conventionally attractive women to advance their MMA careers. I, therefore, cautioned that such an approach not only penalized Black and queer women athletes whose performances of femininity were different than the (white, heterofeminine) "poster girl" image that was most valued in the MMA industry (McClearen 2021), but also reproduced the gender binary and reaffirmed patriarchal gender hierarchies.

Also, in Chapter 4, I examined the circulation of the term, "mom champ," in WMMA, to show how WMMA discourse promotes a "traditional," patriarchal understanding of femininity, characterized by themes of motherhood, maternalism, and "true" womanhood. I also showed how this discourse was supported by prominent WMMA lifestyle brands which promoted a postfeminist "fighter girl" aesthetic, perhaps, best exemplified by the Fight Chix slogan, "Live. Laugh. Love. *Fight*." Taken together, I

argue that the data presented in this study are not consistent with the concept of

"undoing" gender (Deutsch 2007; Risman 2009), but rather, the repackaging of gender in

late capitalism.

BEYOND BREAKING BARRIERS

Reclaiming Empowerment

What does it mean to break barriers? Such language has become so commonplace

in American culture that it seems to have largely escaped critical analysis. How exactly

does one break a barrier? On whose shoulders does the responsibility for this breaking

fall? And how do those who benefit from this breaking experience their emancipation?

Everywhere we look, it seems, women are breaking barriers. At the time of this

writing, Kamala Harris is completing her first term as the United States' first woman vice

president—purportedly "breaking" and "shattering" barriers for every woman who

should follow in her footsteps (Glover 2021; Janes and Wootson Jr. 2020). Yet, women

continue to face barriers in seemingly every institution in the United States and around

the world. For example, just one if four seats in national parliaments are held by women

(World Bank 2021), leaving women severely underrepresented in politics; women in the

workforce are paid, on average, 18 percent less than men (Kochhar 2023) and are

provided fewer opportunities for advancement (Bloch et al. 2021); women in the family

do, on average, three times as much unpaid care and domestic work as men (UN Women

2020) and hold less decision-making power (Moore 2008); and roughly one in three

women are victimized by male violence at some point throughout their lifetime, often at

180

the hands of a family member or intimate partner (Centers for Disease Control and Prevention 2022; World Health Organization 2021). Not surprisingly, these outcomes are even worse for queer women and women of color who bear the brunt of both disproportionately higher rates of poverty and victimization by male and state violence (Bloch et al. 2021; McCown and Platt 2021; Robinson 2020; US Bureau of Labor Statistics 2021; Ussher et al. 2022).

Yet, women *are* increasingly participating in activities that they have not had access to in the past. For instance, women are now serving in infantry roles in the United States military, women are increasingly serving in leadership roles within the Catholic church and other religious institutions, and women are participating as both athletes and officials in sports that have previously been reserved for men. But this comes at a time in which feminism and other social justice movements are under attack in the United States, and women's achievements are becoming further divorced from their political and cultural significance. What, then, does it mean for women in the United States that women are now fighting one another in cages for profit? What is the significance of women's participation in the United States armed forces when those forces are used for the purposes of capitalism, imperialism, and the enriching of the global elite? What is the significance of women's serving in leadership roles in religious institutions if those same institutions prescribe women's second-class status?

If we, as a society, are truly invested in the empowerment of women then we must move beyond neoliberal-postfeminist conceptions of empowerment to address the structures of capitalism, heteropatriarchy, and white supremacy that constrain women's lives. We must move beyond symbolic gestures and achievements and work toward concrete and material gains in women's social, political, and economic status. Most of all, we need to recognize that our current power structure is antithetical to these outcomes and work to dismantle it rather than merely addressing "the fact that women have not benefitted from it" (Kabeer 1994: 20).

Rethinking Women's Empowerment in Sport

Velija, Mierzwinski, and Fortune (2013: 538), in recognizing that the women martial arts athletes in their study were individually "empowered" by physical and mental strength, yet failed to question dominant notions of gendered embodiment and male superiority, ask, "Can this be empowerment?" I argue that it is not. That women become physically stronger through their participation in sport, I argue, is not a revelation. The question is whether that physical power translates into *social* power. In the case of the athletes in this study, it is clear that it does not.

None of the outcomes discussed in this dissertation are consistent with feminist theorizing about empowerment. For the athletes in this study, their MMA training did not appear to correspond with increased physical safety (particularly when you consider the epidemic of IPV in the MMA community), greater freedom of gender and sexual expression, or increased power in their intimate relationships. Perhaps, most importantly, for the athletes in this study, it is clear that their training did not lead to a more critical consciousness. What, then, I ask, is *empowering* about these women's participation in MMA?

Women's sports will consistently fail to serve as sites of empowerment so long as they fail to address the conditions that facilitate women's oppression. As Carol Hanisch famously stated in her essay, "The Personal is Political" (1969: 3), "Women are messed over, not messed up! We need to change the objective conditions, not adjust to them." To presume otherwise is to presume that women are responsible for their own oppression. Feminist sports scholars should reflect carefully on their conceptions of empowerment before deciding whether it is occurring within women's sports. We must be clear in our understanding of the sources of women's oppression and how women's participation in sport addresses these conditions if we are to rescue women's empowerment from its neoliberal-postfeminist façade. While the conditions for empowerment are likely to be debated, assessing these conditions will be the first step in reclaiming empowerment for all.

Toward a Liberatory Martial Arts and Combat Sports

There is an interesting tradition in the sport of Brazilian Jiu-Jitsu known as a "close-out." A close-out is when two athletes—usually from the same team—are set to square off against each other in the finals of a Brazilian Jiu-Jitsu tournament but instead opt *not* to compete against each other for fear of creating undue tension or resentment between the two athletes. Because these tournaments require a winner, the two athletes will then decide amongst themselves who will be awarded the gold medal, with the other athlete *voluntarily giving up their chance to win the tournament* in service of their friendship. While this unique act of solidarity has always stood out to me as a truly selfless act in any otherwise "selfish sport," the greater MMA community's feelings toward close-outs is telling: they *loathe* them. In fact, just recently, the International

Brazilian Jiu-Jitsu Federation (IBJJF) announced that, going forward, athletes who

engaged in close-outs would be penalized both competitively and monetarily (Caulfield

2022). I believe there is a lesson here.

Many people come to martial arts and combat sports, not only for lessons on

punching and kicking, but also for lessons on life. The great 17th century Japanese

swordsman and philosopher, Miyamoto Musashi (2018), wrote that, "The true science of

martial arts means practicing them in such a way that they will be useful at any time, and

to teach them in such a way that they will be useful in all things." Perhaps, it is worth

reconsidering what lessons are being instilled through modern martial arts and combat

sports training. I have encountered many people throughout my time teaching martial arts

who came to the martial arts in search of "discipline," "structure," or the ability to

"compete" in the modern world. Rarely have I encountered individuals looking to

develop greater empathy, solidarity, or a more critical consciousness. We are missing

opportunities to fulfill the liberatory potential of martial arts and combat sports. Rather

than using them in the pursuit of individual gain, we could be using them to build social

consciousness and solidarity. We could be using them to dismantle systems of oppression

and work toward a more just society. We *could* be, but we are *not*.

If martial arts and combat sports are to fulfill their potential as spaces of women's

empowerment, it will require their attention to the structures of capitalism,

heteropatriarchy, and white supremacy that constrain women's lives. It will require their

implementation of anti-capitalist, -sexist, and -racist principles and pedagogies rather than simply providing a space for women to learn how to punch and kick. It will require their decolonization from capitalist, heteropatriarchal, and white supremacist logics and a recognition that women's oppression has been a fundamentally social project. Only then may martial arts and combat sports fulfill their potential as spaces of women's empowerment and combat sports athletes as allies in women's liberation.